Sports Enhancemen
prese

LEARNING GOLF
by
Chuck Hogan

The first golf instruction book specializing in the neurotechnology of learning.

For beginning golfers who want to make the game easy, enjoyable, and satisfying.

For experienced golfers who are not getting what they want from the game.

A system for learning that is quick, clean, and permanent.

Learning Golf was created for the 15-million (and counting) golfers who don't want to WORK at PLAY(ing) a game.

They include:
- Entry-level golfers.
- People starved for time.
- The athletically-undernourished.
- The resurrecting golfer.
- Expert golfers interested in understanding how they got where they are.

Published by Zediker Publishing, Clifton, Colorado, in conjunction with Sports Enhancement Associates, Inc., Sedona, Arizona.

ISBN 0-9624504-4-8

First printing, February, 1993

PRINTED IN THE UNITED STATES OF AMERICA.

Note: in accordance with eligibility requirements for amateur play, none of the models in this book received monetary compensation for their help.

Dedicated to Francis Bartlett Lane and John Blankin and all the others who, in taking up the game of golf, are in for unaccountable frustrations or immense pleasure.

I hope that the contents herein add to the enjoyment of your self as you play golf.

CONTENTS

continued...

B.C.   by johnny hart

FOREWORD

By T.J. Tomasi

The book you are about to read is one of a kind, both in its conception and its presentation. It was conceived from the union of a fertile mind and a pressing problem. The fertile mind is that of Chuck Hogan, golf professional, teacher, and philosopher. The pressing problem came to light after a lesson many years ago, when a beginning student said to Hogan, "That was great, but when are you going to teach me to play the game of golf?" Most instructors would have ignored this comment, but Hogan realized that the student was correct, he hadn't taught her how to play the game of golf, only how to swing the club. It was at that point that Chuck Hogan became an iconoclast, forging a new road in golf instruction, the map of which you have in your hands.

This book presents a new model for learning the game of golf, constructed from the most up-to-date research from the physical and social sciences, focused through your author's many years of experience as a teacher of the game.

This effort has made Chuck Hogan an innovator in golf instruction and as such he has set a rocky road for himself. No person who introduces a new learning model is welcome by the intellectual squatters who have already staked out the territory. The sequence is universal as the innovation evolves. First the powers that be ignore it. Then as the innovation grabs hold at the grass roots level, they argue that it has no validity. And, when it becomes obvi-ous that the innovation will be a suc-cess, they claim to have invented it.

While this book is ostensibly about golf, what it is really about is our lives as learners, adapters, and enjoyers of life. Hogan himself has a high regard for man's potential but a low regard for man's current perfor-mance. He is an existentialist in that his learning model places the indi-vidual (you) at the center of the learn-ing paradigm and as the process unfolds, he shows you how to create your own game, judged by your own standards of success and failure.

To Hogan, first and last, golf is a game, and that game is to be played for enjoyment.

Unfortunately, if you've played enough golf, you probably have a suspicion that there is more to the game than you are currently experi-encing. To many, golf is a rendezvous with anxiety. You come to the course excited with the expectation of enjoy-ment but finish your "game" feeling and looking like you've just been to a war. And once the shell shock of fail-ure has worn off, you're back on the practice tee doing hard time for a really "hard" game.

The model presented here proves that golf is not a hard game to learn because golfers, as human beings, are perfect learners. The problem is that golfers have been seduced to follow a faulty learning model where swing mechanics has staked out center stage, kept there by the legions of teaching pros, books, and golf magazines scrambling for a piece of the multi-billion dollar golf market. In effect, they have collabo-rated to convince the golf public that correct swing mechanics inevitably equals good golf. This, despite the fact that no player of quality has ever played well by thinking about swing mechanics while they swing, and conversely, almost every poor player thinks themselves to death.

Good players concentrate on making a smooth swing or they visualize and become integrated with the target, but they never think about what their knees or elbows are doing. When asked about his downswing thought, Tom Kite, currently golf's all-time leading money winner, responded with a useful oxymoron, "I think about nothing."

Having said this, please understand that the positioning of swing mechanics in their rightful place in the hierarchy of learning to play golf doesn't mean that you can play good golf with any old swing, however bad it may be.

Thus, while the Hogan model takes you to the next level of learning to play golf, there is an excellent section on how to swing the club.

Who should read this book?

This book is perfect for beginners, who as far as golf is concerned, are a blank slate, free from the bad feelings and habits already wired into most experienced golfers. Hogan's learning model will insulate the beginner from all the things that historically have slowed the golfer's development.

But the learning model is also for the already tainted, the experienced golfer who has a head filled with the gremlins of golf instruction. Golfers are notoriously promiscuous in that they will lie down with any swing theory that comes along. This sends them down a patchwork of blind

alleys and instills a swirling confusion that is never resolved. For them, this book will serve as a rewiring blueprint that will keep them focused as they rebuild their game.

Most golfers are looking for a secret, a shortcut, one mystical word that will open the treasure box of good golf. When I was teaching, I hung a sign that said "4 Lessons—$100, 1 Lesson—$1000." And when a student asked why one lesson was a thousand dollars, I would explain, "If you want magic, you have to pay for it."

But in truth, there is a magical source available to us because we all have within us our own genie with the power to grant us the wish of good golf. What our host, Chuck Hogan, shows us in this book, is how to summon that genie to create and preserve our enjoyment of this great game we all love so much—and isn't that really what magic is all about?

T.J. Tomasi is the Instruction Editor for Golf Illustrated *magazine.*

8

Choose to have fun.

Action yields
results.

Fun creates
enjoyment.

Knowledge
facilitates action.

Enjoyment invites
participation.

Insight generates
knowledge.

Participation
focuses attention.

Awareness
promotes insight.

Attention expands
awareness.

Follow this progression of aptitude clockwise.*

This is what you are about to embark on—a journey toward learning golf that will be both fun and rewarding.

*From O.B. Shallow.

INTRODUCTIONS
A few answers to a few questions.

i.
WHY THIS BOOK
AND THIS APPROACH
A new book for a new golfer.

Get and use this book because you deserve it!

The world of advanced education strategies recognizes that there are no broken, stupid, or hopeless students. What exists are unique people with differing motivations and different instructional needs.

Anyone can learn anything if the instruction is presented in small enough chunks and is presented with respect to the student's learning and sensory style.

This book presents the learning of golf in a way that allows you to learn quickly, cleanly, and permanently. Every fundamental golfing skill is made clear and precise. Each is presented in a way that accommodates different learning styles.

Your learning will be permanent because every chunk will be experienced by you in a form that is rele-vant to you. The fundamentals will be both "fun" and "mental." This book is about *how* to learn as much as *what* to learn.

The benefit to you will be proficiency from the beginning and a potential for as much improvement as you desire.

Most importantly, herein is a lifetime of self-enjoyment as you recreate through the game of golf.

ii.
DEFINITIONS
Who might you be?

Entry level.

So you're taking up golf... You've heard that you should take lessons, or you'll be taught by a spouse or friend. Okay, fine, but please read and use this book first. Save money, time, and mountains of frustration. Believe me. Save a life(time) that is near and dear—yours.

Starved for time.

Yes, you must play "corporate golf" to elevate your image and earnings. You just don't have the six hours a day and the dedication that you've heard is required for golf. This book is the route to looking good and scoring reasonably well in the shortest period of time and with the least amount of sweat on your part. Impress your friends and clients and get what you want sooner than later!

The athletically-undernourished.

I cringe every time I hear a professional instructor comment that the student is "an athletic klutz" or "isn't motivated to work." The fact is that you are motivated. The fact is also that your brain is simply lacking appropriate stored references for it to direct precise motor skills. This book will give you those references in a way that makes you look and play like a veteran.

The resurrecting golfer.

After dozens of lessons, bushels of books and videos, and countless tips, you remain as confused as ever, playing the same or worse as you did three years ago. You have one hundred times more tips than you need. What you want is less information and more *knowledge*. You just want to "do it"—hit the ball to the target.

Play golf.

Expert golfers who want to understand how they got where they are.

There is an ironic lesson to be learned from the professional golfers who define the standards of play: the successful touring professional did not follow the "common practice" of investing his time in the tip-of-the-day club (or at least he resigned his charter long ago). The touring professional learned through experience in *exactly* the same way that the athletically-undernourished did. The only difference was in the meaning of the experiences.

It isn't *what* you learned. It is *how* it was presented to you and how it was processed by you. This book will make it simple again. You will be free to *play* golf. Take a few weeks and transform work into play. After all, recreation is *re-creation*.

iii.
PASSING GO

And collecting what is rightfully yours.
(For resurrecting golfers only.)

Let's say you purchased this book because you want to relearn golf. *Good idea!*

It is a good idea because this book is about learning golf, which also makes it about *re*-learning golf.

You may have committed 5, 10, 15, or more years in pursuit of golf proficiency. Now you can do it in a matter of months, maybe weeks. Through this text you will find out where you "went wrong." And what you will discover is that you never actually went wrong. You went exactly right—given the nature and direction of your efforts.

Learning Golf unfolds a systematic approach to mastering the fundamentals of golf. But it is far more than "getting back to the basics."

This is all there is!

There are no more fundamentals to learn beyond those presented in this book. Yes, a par-shooter possesses numerous "advanced" skills. However, these are skills that, literally, have been advanced. They were advanced in the course of playing the game. It is a mistake to believe that this book is only a stepping-stone to learning more mechanics in the future. It is instead a vehicle that will take you as far as you wish to go.

Relearning golf is not a matter of "forgetting" everything you know. No offense, but you didn't know it in the first place. Or, more precisely, you knew it but you didn't *recognize* your knowledge of it.

If you've been around golf for a while, you have, at one time, known exactly what you needed to know to get on with the game. The problem is that you have known too much. So much that you were not able to commit your trust to one set of things that could define your mechanics.

Indecision was the only culprit. *Indecision:* the byproduct of the intellectually-confused mind. *Indecision is the life-blood of golf instruction.* Every magazine, most teachers, and the vast majority of programs and materials dealing in the instruction process, all feed on indecision. If it weren't for indecision you wouldn't be reading these words now.

It has been said that only the ignorant can play great golf. That is somewhat true, and it's a real compliment. The root word is "ignore." It is a great gift to ignore all the possible swing theories and techniques and tips that you've been exposed to and simply be centered and decisive about your own game. Can you imagine where Jack Nicklaus would be if he approached every shot wondering which swing to use?

In all likelihood, you learned the opposite of *ignore*-ance. You bought the books, magazines, and videos, took the lessons, listened to the tips. You now have more options available than Chevrolet®.

Instead of standing over the ball with one clear objective, you are filing through a dozen things that you must do "right."

Instead of relying on tips and multiple mechanics, you'll now find it much more efficient and satisfying to learn one basic model. You may have also realized that the latest magazine article or the newest tip did, indeed, improve your play for a time. That is because your mind, for the duration that it was focused on the advice, was cleared of indecision.

Focusing clearly and precisely on one model has the same effect as the tip in that it, too, reduces the searching and sorting. The difference is that the model stays with you while the tip fades away. The model eliminates confusion and frees your brain from overload. Take the time and make the commitment to learning what is in this book. Use either learning process to install the skill permanently and with clarity and then operate from the purity of that source. You will have built a solid base which you can come back to under all conditions. Tips and "thinkering" give way to a singular pattern, easy to repeat.

Don't get down on yourself for your "past life" as a golfer. Instead congratulate yourself for being a great learner! You learned all these options from the instruction industry that surrounds you. Your subconscious mind is like a genie that simply grants whatever you wish for. Your genie simply said "Yes" to whatever you asked it for. You might not like the results of the learning, but the learning itself was efficient. And if you can learn what you don't want —indecision—then you can also learn to be decisive. All you have to do is to ask and then act congruently. Ask for what is in this book. It is all that you need. Ignore the rest. And good luck to you. You have earned it!

Note: For a few answers to a few questions of another kind, consult the *Glossary* on page 161.

B.C.   by johnny hart

NON-GOLF technical and mechanical skills	**GOLF** target integration speed, courtesy, and safety
Preswing ————————————	**Putting**
grip stance aim & alignment	
Swing ————————————	**Putting,** procedures, rules, and etiquette
Centeredness of hit ————————————	**Chipping**
(fit of equipment)	
Full shots (all clubs) ————————————	**Pitch/Sand**

GOLF

Study this schematic for learning golf. On the left are all the precursors to playing golf. On the right are all the things that teach you golf. The list on the right also has simple mechanical skills, but the real knowledge is in the experience—learning by doing.

CHAPTER I
WHAT IS GOLF?
And what is it not?

Most "golf" lessons and most "golf" tips are a misnomer. *They are not about "golf."* They are all about some precursor or component of golf which *can* lead to playing golf.

Actual, real, honest *golf* is the adventure of being on the course. A golf shot is interaction with a target and its conditions. You are a part of those conditions, not separate from them. You are one piece of the entire activity. You are playing golf when you are being absorbed in the interaction of literally playing with and through the target. There is no self-awareness at an intellectual level when you are playing and interacting with the target. There is only a sensory experience in which your awareness merges and blends with the doing. You just "do it."

Golf swing is golf swing. It is something to learn in preparation to play golf. But it is certainly *not* golf! When playing "golf swing," your awareness is not devoted to a target. Your attention is focused inward on some mechanical motion which

attempts to satisfy some or all notions of how to swing a golf club.

The same may be said for all the other pre-golf components. Learning the mechanics of chip, pitch, sand, putting, and specialty shots is not golf. These components are each important pieces in the "getting-ready-to-golf" formula.

This is a very important concept. When you play golf, just play golf. Here's you, here's the ball, there's the target. Go to it. Hit the ball to the target as best you can. Find the ball and do it again. *Experience, adjust, experience, adjust...* The golf course is made for playing a game! So go there and PLAY golf.

Learn all the components of golf *off* the course. Practice the techniques and develop the skills on the practice range, putting green, or in the backyard, garage, or living room.

Learning to type is one analogy. You learn the components first: hand position, key position, use of the machine, and etc. Those are all precursors to typing. You practice and

15

learn these mechanics so your mind will be free to focus on typing: transferring words from one page to another. The same is true for learning to drive a car or learning to write. It cannot be different in golf if you are to learn quickly, precisely, and efficiently.

Keep it straight in your mind. You can PLAY golf or practice components, but not at the same time. Choose one or the other. When you play golf, PLAY. When you practice golf, put your energy into accomplishing the task at hand. The two will blend without your conscious awareness as your mastery unfolds. Just enjoy the process.

CHAPTER 2
TO GOLF
OR NOT TO GOLF

It is *the question...*

These questions often arise:

1.   Should I play golf while I am learning the fundamentals?
2.   Wouldn't I be better off just practicing at home or on the range?
3.   Don't I run the risk of confusion when I am on the course and trying to learn at the same time?

Answer: Playing golf and learning golf fundamentals are two entirely different things and events. Do each as separate activities deserving of their own attention and use of your energy.

Playing golf is an act of *intelligence.* Learning golf fundamentals is an act of *intellect.* Do both, but not at the same time and/or in the same environment.

Go play golf. Go to the golf course. Hit the ball. Find the ball. Repeat until the ball is in the hole. Have fun. *The End.*

Learn the fundamentals. One chunk at a time. Do this in the back yard, living room, or driving range, but NOT on the golf course. Put your intention and attention on each chunk, one at a time. Continue until you have claimed mastery of each successive chunk and have validated your success.

Keep playing golf. Your mastery of fundamentals will merge into your golf game as an act of play, not by forcing it there with your will. "All intelligence arises from concrete to abstract."*

Play golf with the indulgence of a child and your fundamentals will fall into place without your conscious awareness. It is possible to notice improvement only in retrospect.

*From *The Magical Child,* a book by Joseph Chilton Pearce.

HEY!!! WHATTABOUT GOLF?

Impatience may be among us. So hurry up and read this!

So you wanted to learn golf and here you are doing the laborious stuff. You haven't even gotten to hit a ball yet!

Okay. *Learn golf.* Go to the putting green (the one at the course or in your living room). Start putting. Skip to Chapter 12.f for some ideas.

The putting green is a microcosm of the golf course. Get involved with the ball, target, rules, procedures, etiquette, and protocols on the putting green. All of this is the "golf" part of learning golf. As you progress through the non-golf fundamentals of pre-swing, full-swing, and centeredness of contact, you can at the same time (but in a different environment) be learning golf. These two "realms" will merge appropriately to make you a "golfer" in only a few weeks.

CHAPTER 3
YOU ARE A
PERFECT LEARNER

*A dumb person can learn in one day
what it takes a smart monkey a lifetime
to learn.**

*Moshe Feldenkreis, one genius in the pioneering of learning, offers this metaphor for the immense learning capacity of the human brain.

The human brain with its 50 to 100 billion learning cells has up to 600,000 connecting links per cell, also capable of processing information. It is all quite incomprehensible. At the very least, you are incredible as an information processor.

Consider this enormous potential as testimony of the capacity that you have for learning anything you want. Even the slightest grasp of understanding of your learning potential will shift your attitude to one of eager anticipation. You CAN learn anything!

It may be that you have previously *learned* to feel unathletic or inadequate as you endeavored in athletic motor skills. Your *learning* may have been one of intimidation, embarrassment, or exclusion when you attempted to play games with others. Maybe Mom didn't want you to be a tomboy or Dad thought games got in the way of work or "serious" needs. Maybe your autonomic sympathetic nervous system (a fancy way to describe the mechanism which moves away from pain) disallowed your athletic participation. Athletics may have been emotionally painful for you. The message was, "ouch, that hurts," so you don't do it anymore. Smart brain!

19

There are a million ways in which you could *learn* to be disadvantaged or undernourished in athletic skill development. Simply understanding that you *learned* NOT to develop athletic/motor-skill representations in your brain does not make you a victim. It makes you a learner! A PERFECT learner. If you can *learn* that, you can *learn* anything! You are—everyone is—a learner of magnificent proportions.

Now that you have decided to *learn* golf (to exercise a birthright of choice), all you need is:

1. *A system for learning.*
   (found in this book)
2. *Patience.*
   (nurtured by your brain)
3. *Self-nurturing.*
   (generated by your brain)

CHAPTER 4
YOUR BOOK,
YOUR GAME,
YOUR BUSINESS

*Don't tell anyone
that you're doing this.*

"No, no, no, your left hand has to be like this! I told you to keep your head down. Keep your left arm straight. Swing straight back. Greg Norman does it this way. The only way to putt is like this. You used the wrong club. Look, I'm the pro so I must know what I am talking about..."

This list is endless.

As soon as you announce (either implicitly or explicitly) that you are "taking up golf"—even if you have already been playing for 20 years—you open yourself up to a deluge of advice. Nearly all the advice should be shunned. Even the two-bits worth that is good advice will be overwhelmed into obscurity by the volume of bad advice. The intention of the advisors is good, but the result to you is overload.

How would you like to attempt the learning of typing with seventy-one teachers giving you their ideas of how it's done? Do you think you might get confused? Believe me,

there are far more than seventy-one golf instructors who will enter your life. Beware of free advice—it's worth less than its cost. (Beware, as well, of advice that costs...)

Keeping a "low profile" doesn't mean that you are blind to observing success. You should observe and model what other successful golfers are doing. Try it. If it works, keep doing it. If it doesn't work, don't do it. Don't ever try to *make* it work. The advice in this paragraph applies after you have learned and mastered the fundamentals in this text.

The basic rule is this: *Beware everyone bearing gifts.*

21

CHAPTER 5
GOLF
The game.

Is golf difficult or is it the way it's taught that makes it so tough?

After a year or two of playing golf, you will discover that there is no such thing as a golfer who is not also a golf instructor. Oh yes. Everyone has a tip which is going to help you, possibly even put you at one with the universe. *"Keep your head down"* is one such cardinal offering.

The reason for this may be that everyone's "answers" to golf have always been found through subjective notions, not to mention inductive reasoning. That is to say that just because one idea works for one golfer, it must, therefore, work for *all* golfers. So this one golfer offers his or her prescription to anyone who will listen.

Another reason is that the best players in the world become the models for every golfer. Forget that you only play once a week, rarely think of golf between rounds, have wholly different motivations for playing, and a totally different concept of the game—to name a few differences between you and Greg Norman. However, you will still get much of the same instructional input as he does.

Mostly, however, the reason that golf has become such a difficult game to learn is because there is *so much stuff* to learn. With all the additions to the instructional theory, swing design, and "tip" pool made over the last 300 years, we find ourselves overwhelmed with thousands of do's and don'ts. At the same time, there has been very little mention of *how to learn* all this stuff. Golf has been saturated with the "whats" and starved for the "hows" to learn the whats.

Just look around at the explosion of golf instruction books, videos, and magazines. The *what* to learn is expanding like the national debt. There are heaps and gobs of material on what to do when you swing, or what to do during any portion of the swing, regardless of how miniscule that portion may be! Every millisecond of the swinging motion has been dissected, analyzed, and cobbled back together in countless combinations. These puzzle pieces have been scattered out and then forced to fit back together.

If some of the pieces don't fit the way they should, no problem: trim them down, hammer them in, or paste them up. Doesn't work. Many golf instructors attempt mismatched resurrections that would pale the life work of Dr. Frankenstein, creating endlessly more puzzles.

And the worse it gets, the worse it gets. That is the nature of a monster. There is certainly more competition in the instructional marketplace for producing "stuff to do" than there is for producing materials that will improve the "stuff" to do it with.

Granted, much of the new "stuff" is a rehash of previously-published "stuff," but this spiralling parody rarely clarifies or makes the mastery of the subject easier. It more often adds to the confusion, thereby propagating even more "stuff" on the subject.

With the constant and expanding content of "stuff," the student of the game is overwhelmed with possibilities. Confusion is difficult, if not impossible, to avoid. Golf becomes an exercise in analytical regurgitation rather than an immersion in intuitive pleasure.

The game was not meant for the consumption of content.

It was made for the freedom of mind and body to bond with an environment in which the game can be fully *played*. It is in the playing itself where the real learning can and should take place.

Golf is not a difficult game!

How can a *game* be difficult? By definition, games are made for play. *Play* is the opposite of *work*, which is, by definition, the act of trying and efforting. Play is for rejuvenation, regeneration, recreation (re-creation), and self-expansion.

The rule is this: If you are not invited to PLAY, then don't do it.

In the words of O. B. Shallow:

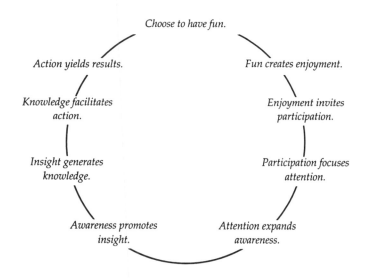

Choose to have fun.

Action yields results.

Fun creates enjoyment.

Knowledge facilitates action.

Enjoyment invites participation.

Insight generates knowledge.

Participation focuses attention.

Awareness promotes insight.

Attention expands awareness.

Study this cycle of internally-generated motivation. There are those who say that hard work is the key to success. That may be true, but only in terms of time and energy expenditure (aka: dedication). If the fun and enjoyment aren't there, the hard work will yield hesitation, frustration, demotivation, and bitterness. In some way, shape, or form—in *any and every* way, shape, or form—it must be fun or it will not work.

Fun is your own creation.

Create your own fun.

That is all you need:

Eloquent simplicity.

CHAPTER 6
HOW TO
CONFUSE THE
HUMAN BRAIN

Read this number:

6027735421.

Now close your eyes and repeat the number. How did you do?

Try this number:

542547984.

Close your eyes and repeat.

Now try it this way:

602-773-5421

(as in a telephone number). Or:

542-54-7984

(as in a Social Security number).

Do you find that they're now easier to remember and repeat? Do you find one set of numbers confusing, while the other set is relatively easier to learn and remember?

While the human brain is incredibly and incomprehensibly vast in its processing capacity (the brain has at least 50 to 100 billion neurons or thinking cells activated by bio-chemical electrical patterns moving incredibly fast), the conscious mind becomes confused when it is overloaded. Overloading occurs when there is too much "stuff" being consciously processed at one time. One example is too many numbers (such as 6027735421). But when the numbers are broken into chunks (602-773-3421) the confusion is reduced or eliminated.

Learning becomes much easier.

Golf instruction or "thinking" about the golf shot at hand can be an overload. For example, you may be getting ready by thinking: "Let's see, the instructor or magazine said: 'grip, knees flexed, arms hanging, start back with arms, slow back, straight left arm, turn, lift, shift weight, etc., etc.'" This type of processing can and will make anyone look and feel like a failure. But it is not failure; it is simply an information overload.

Another excellent way to confuse the brain is to input information in a manner that the brain cannot accept. Each of you has a predominant means by which you gain understanding or comprehension of instruction. This is referred to as a learning "bias."

25

Some people's brains learn best by seeing how something works. These people might prefer a demonstration or detailed photographs of the golf swing. Others learn best through messages that come from their sense of touch or tactile association with the task at hand. They may gain understanding, for example, through analogies to related activities they're more familiar with. Still others learn best by hearing a description of the activity or through rhythmic patterns of motion. Those who learn through listening may prefer cassette tapes or lectures to the printed word. Those who learn through their sense of rhythm or patterns of motion (called "auditory" learners), may, for example, respond fully only when the combined sequence of each golf swing position is clear.

An instructor must be aware of the learning bias of a student. Otherwise, the information may be perfectly correct but the meaning may be lost. When deprived of the *appropriate* sensory input—that which induces the brain to learn—confusion is automatic.

Virtually everyone learns quickly and permanently when they are *fully engaged* in the experience of the activity. Experience occurs when all three senses (see, feel, hear) are involved simultaneously. *Experience* is what makes the activity relevant to the brain, giving meaning to the activity beyond a simple intellectual articulation. Relevancy is experience. Experience is instant learning.

A third way to confuse the learner is to offer information to the person's brain in a way it is unable to comprehend. Some people learn through explanation, articulation, symbolism, sequence, and analyzation. A CPA is apt to be this kind of learner. Others learn better in a random, concrete (hands-on), intuitive, non-verbal manner. An artist is likely to be in this group.

Finally, a great way to make a human appear to be a klutz is to assume that everyone learns at the same rate. Of course we do not all learn at the same rate. Each of us learns at our unique pace.

By following the process of learning presented in this text, and by indulging in the exercises, you will find that there will be minimal confusion and maximum learning efficiency. You will avoid a confused brain. All the fundamentals which lead to proficient golf have been broken into small chunks. Master one chunk at a time and move to the next.

Each exercise will accommodate your unique sensory system as well as your learning bias. Move at your own rate. Be your own judge. Enjoy the process. Enjoy *yourself*...

CHAPTER 7
ABOUT
LEARNING...
And learning golf.

All behaviors—good, bad, and indifferent—are learned.

This book is about learning golf.

The concern, therefore, is that you learn behaviors that help you advance a golf ball around a golf course. This advancement, of the ball and your ability, depends on learning behaviors that are correct, consistent, and satisfying. A behavior will be correct if the source the behavior is modeled after is correct. A behavior will be consistent if optional behaviors are minimum or, better yet, non-existent. A behavior is a habit. This book will instill in you the habit of great golf, played in its purest form. A behavior will be satisfying or not by your judgement alone.

It all has to do with learning. Learning what you wish to learn.

The Cycle of Competence.   27

There are two kinds of learning. First is the kind of

learning that allows you to be able to DO something. Riding a bike is one example. The other kind of learning allows you to be able to talk about what you learned. Writing a bicycle maintenance book might be that kind of learning. One is action; the other is analysis.

Unless you want to become a golf instructor, the best kind of learning for you to engage in is the first kind. You don't want to talk about *how* to golf. You want to be able to play golf at a level which is enjoyable and satisfying for you.

To learn in a manner that allows you to "do it," you simply need to follow a pattern of learning.

You have, perhaps without knowing, followed this pattern to learn hundreds of things. It is how you learned to do anything you do with competence. In those areas where you lack competence, it is because the pattern was broken for one reason or another.

This pattern is called the *Cycle of Competence*. Here is how it works.

Step 1. *Perceive the model.*
Step 2. *Repetition.*
Step 3. *Habituation.*
Step 4. *Variation.*

There is no reason that learning golf, or learning anything else for that matter, should be difficult.

All you have to do is follow the Cycle of Competence:

Step 1. Decide on a model that you will follow to learn the components of golf. Don't proceed until your model is appealing, singular, and clear to you.

Step 2. Repeat the perfect activity of the model as suggested in the next chapter.

Step 3. Make this activity a habit and claim that habit as your own. Two different methods for doing that are soon to follow.

Step 4. Now vary the activity of the skill as called for by the variation in the environment of golf (eg. different distances, ball lie, weather, etc.). This is the part that is really exciting and engaging. This is the part that is really *golf.*

The variations are what you learn through practice. Each variation is a unique experience. These experiences are stored in your infinite resource bin, the subconscious mind. They will be there when you need them; all you have to do is ask!

How could you mess up the Cycle of Competence when it comes to golf?

Easy, it is built into the system...

Step 1 can be messed up if you:

Get going before you have a clear, singular model.

Change models frequently.

Have multiple models or try to do too many things at once.

Get into variation before you have habituation.

Step 2 sabotage occurs if:

Your repetitions of the activity you wish to learn are haphazard or imprecise relative to your model.

You don't do the repetitions at all. You might not make it fun and quit because it becomes work.

You don't reward yourself for your efforts and quit.

Step 3 comes to a halt if:

You fail to realize that your habit is a habit (when it is, in fact, a habit). You can know it is a habit if you do the same thing every time without thought. That's a good definition of "habit." When you get to that point—when you know that your habit is, indeed, a habit—be sure to acknowledge and celebrate your confirmation of this achievement.

Step 4 will destroy the process if:

You experiment with variation before you have habituation.

Do not worry about moving into variation until you are well-experienced at *playing* the game. Believe me, the course and its conditions will teach you what to do and when to do it. Just be open to its suggestions—after you have fully completed the first three steps. The whole trick is to avoid getting Step 4 ahead of the first three. This is critical!

Do not go onto Step 4 until you are finished, done, and over with the three steps that precede!

Following in the next chapter are two ways that the Cycle can be put into effect to learn what you wish to learn.

CHAPTER 8 LEARNING METHODS

We mean the means.

There are two methods that will enable you to learn anything you wish to learn. Both allow the Cycle of Competence to run its full course. They are the 3-STEP and 21-DAY methods. Both work equally well, but one will work best for you.

Try the 3-STEP method first. It is the fastest and easiest way to learn. The 3-STEP method won't work for everyone (actually, it really will work for everyone provided that they can accept that it will work...).

The 3-STEP method.

You have used this 3-STEP method to learn hundreds of skills that long ago reached the level of automatic—tying your shoes, riding a bike, shaving, to name a few. This process was employed at the *implicit* level; all the "work" went on under the surface. It is also possible to apply this process at the *explicit* level to learn anything that you wish to learn. The reason the 3-STEP process won't work for everyone is because not everyone will accept its efficiency.

Something that is set out to be learned—golf for instance—is of sufficient importance that some people believe they must put in their time and effort to *earn* the skill. Beliefs are very powerful. Some people believe learning requires work. Some believe learning is easy. Both are correct.

For those who refuse to believe in the 3-STEP method, then there is the 21-DAY habituation process. It also won't work for everyone. The 21-DAY method is hard to stick to for those who would be best off using the 3-STEP method. Both have exactly the same effect and produce the same "quality" of learning. The real difference is that the 3-STEP method is relatively "effortless" learning, while the actions that lead to installment of the skill using the 21-DAY process are somewhat more "efforted." So there you have it.

The 3-STEP method will become very familiar to you as you progress through the fundamentals in this book. It will be reiterated and applied to each chunk of instructional material presented. Because of this presentation, the 3-STEP method will appear to be the preferred method, and it is. If it will work for you, and chances are very good that it will, then use it.

Although the 3-STEP method may sound too easy to ever possibly be effective, rest assured that it works. After experiencing its effectiveness, you'll understand that previous beliefs you may have held about attaining proficiency were, in themselves, what held you back. Ideas like Edison's famous *genius is 1-percent inspiration and 99-percent perspiration*, are exactly backward for those who apply the 3-STEP method!

Given an understanding of the perfect learning blueprint we all possess, you will see that inspiration, focused in the right direction, will do you just as much good as perspiration, and possibly a whole lot more.

Focused inspiration is the key to resolving the paradox between what you want to do and what you do. What is necessary is successful *negotiation* between the conscious mind (that which desires) and the subconscious mind (that which does). The 3-STEP and 21-DAY methods accomplish exactly that. With this congruency or permission in place, what you get is what you want.

The 3-STEP method is as simple as:
1. See the model.
2. See yourself as the model.
3. Feel the model.

All you need to do is to follow the process *precisely* and you will have quick, clean, efficient, and *per-*

The 3-STEP learning method. Step 1: *See the model.* In this example, it's Ben Hogan, one of the truly great players. Step 2: *See yourself as the model.* Put your face, clothing, and body on the model. Step 3: *Be the model.* Now it's you! 31

The absolute most critical thing is to not get any step ahead of the others. You must be able to see a fully "glitchless" picture in your mind before moving on.

manent mastery of the skill you wish to acquire.

But being precise has a few parameters: First, be *discriminating*. The 3-STEP process works. Be careful what you ask for because you might get it. With the 3-STEP process, you *will* get it! You could use this process to learn 500 different swing mechanics and end up a babbling idiot. The entire point would have then been missed. Stay true to a *singular, clear, and precise* model.

Second, *follow the steps without deviation!* To go to Step 2 before Step 1 is one-hundred-percent clear, clean, and finished in your mind is to cheat yourself. If you do so, you'll think that the 3-STEP process does not work.

In more detail:

Step 1. *See the model.*

Find a model that is appealing and suitable to you. If not the model presented in this text, then find some man or woman out there who appeals to you and seems appropriate—in other words, one who, by your judgement, presents him- or herself as the picture of a fully competent golfer. Fred Couples or Cindy Rarick would be better choices than a high-handicap golfer. Choose a model that has a similar physical structure to yours. The only important factors are that the model is appealing, appropriate, and available.

View the model, over and over in your mind, from a *disassociated state* —you are on the outside looking in. Your model possesses what you believe are perfect golfing mechanics.

View and review until the picture of the model is pervasive and "glitchless" in your mind.

Pervasive means that this picture is the only picture you access whenever you consider the mechanical skill you're learning; it arises spontaneously every time you formally or casually think of the skill.

Glitchless means that your picture of the model's mechanics is clear, vivid, and singular. There are no foggy, muted, overlapping, or contaminated characteristics in the picture in your mind. You can see every detail in perfect clarity. An example of a glitch would be seeing the perfect action three times and then witness the action change or lose detail on the fourth.

When—and only when—you have a disassociated, pervasive, and glitchless picture of the model in your mind, you are then ready to move to Step 2.

Step 2. *See yourself as the model.*

Everything here is the same as Step 1 except that now the model has your face on it. You remain in a disassociated state, and the activity of the model is exactly the same.

Just like adjusting the fine tuning controls on your television set, the picture is now getting clearer, sharper, and brighter in your mind. There are evermore details and familiarity as you visualize the action.

You are ready to progress to Step 3 when—and only when—your mind is processing a disassociated, pervasive, and glitchless picture in your mind. When you are fully satisfied that you have accomplished Step 2, then move to the final step.

Step 3. *Feel the model. Become the model.*

Up to this point, all activity has been from a disassociated perspective. Now it is time to *associate* by stepping into the model. You now have the club in your hand and you are actually performing the activity you have been visualizing.

It is *extremely* important that you do not attempt the "physical" action of the skill until Step 3.

You can now *feel* everything that you were seeing in Steps 1 and 2. You are on the inside looking out. You not only feel and register these senses "physically" but also emotionally—you experience the exhilaration of mastering the skill. You have arrived!

There is a fourth step: *Validate and graduate!*

This step must always follow any process of learning. Formally acknowledge that you are done with this piece of learning. Send yourself a clear, strong message that you have mastered the skill. This step is missing from most attempts at learning. If you don't acknowledge that you have learned the skill, you may continue to pursue the skill, and that doesn't make sense at any level. It's the absence of this step, along with inexact representations of the skill by the learner, that have led to the old idea that you always must "work on the fundamentals." Not so. You've got it!

Validate and graduate using the means provided in this book at the conclusion of each fundamental skills section.

The 3-STEP process takes as long as it takes. Some people will progress through all three steps in a matter of days, even hours. Young children do it all the time. They will quickly imprint a perfectly clear picture in Step 1 and easily see their face in Step 2. They will find that the performance of Step 3 is accurate and proficient.

Other people of the "left-brain" orientation will think that this is all "too easy." The analytical/intellectual types have a nagging suspicion that learning cannot result through a simple matter of relying on their brains. And as always, their brains are correct! If doubt lingers—if you don't believe you have "gotten it" by following the 3-STEP process—that is an indication of incongruency. Your subconscious mind and nervous system are not prepared to accept the reality that learning has taken place. These people must gain their *permission* through perspiration and hard work.

No problem. Go to work...

Here is your alternative.

The 21-DAY habituation process.

This alternative works equally as well as the 3-STEP method. It requires more time and effort, but for those who believe in the "work ethic," the 21-DAY method will satisfy their minds that they have earned ownership of the skill they set out to learn.

Through the 21-DAY method you are selectively and systematically installing specific habits.

Step 1. Determine why you want to learn the skill.

You must achieve conceptual appreciation of the necessity of learning this skill. This is as simple as

33

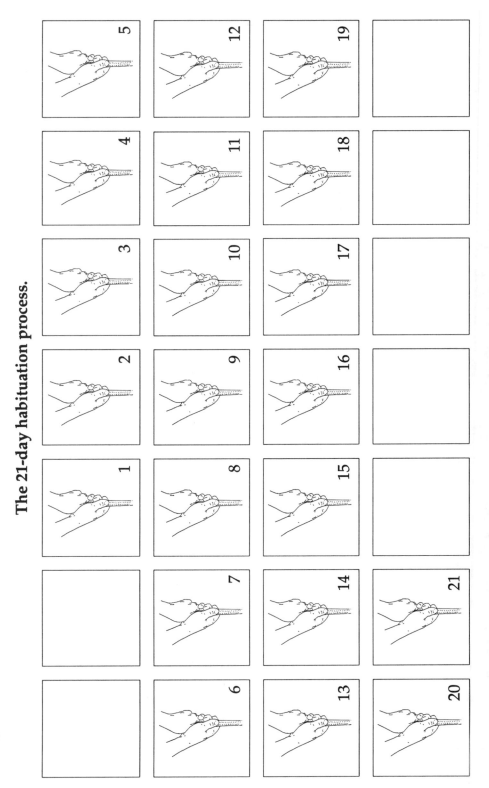

The 21-day habituation process.

acknowledging that the fundamental must be mastered. You must develop a complete, systematic, and functional set of golf mechanics.

Step 2. Determine exactly how to accomplish the task.

You must determine how you will know when you are doing it right. Is it from comparing yourself with the illustrations and photos, or from realizing the sensations that are described in the text? Either way, make a determination. You must provide your brain with precise information.

Step 3. Now for the process...

Execute at least 60 repetitions of the skill per day for 21 consecutive days. Put your full intent and attention into each repetition of the skill.

Focus all your energy into each repetition. Each must be precise, perfect, and clear. This is equivalent to the glitchless visualization of 3-STEP. Each repetition must be glitchless; a glitch is a mistake in performing the skill in a repetition.

You can split the repetitions into many small sets in order to maintain full concentration. For example, do 12 sets of 5 repetitions or 5 sets of 12.

After 21 days of 60 repetitions per day, you've got it! The new skill is no longer new. It is now a habit and will be "with you" until you choose to replace it with another following the same process.

Note: You can practice and install more than one skill during any 21-day block as long as each skill receives your full and total concentration and commitment.

Step 4. Validate and graduate.

This is the same as for the 3-STEP process. Make the decision and commitment to being done, finished, and proclaim yourself master of the skill. If you have followed the process precisely, the skill is habituated.

Why bother?

Okay. We're asking you to do a few things in this chapter that may seem complex and unnecessary. But they are the essence of simplicity and are most definitely necessary. Without following these steps, what you have in your hands is a good book filled with golf instruction. However, if you follow the information in this book with the steps for learning, validating, and graduating then you have a great way for learning golf!

Golf is an easy game when it is *made* easy by following specific learning strategies and processes.

After you've used one of these learning models to master all fundamental components, that does not mean that every ball will fly perfectly and every shot will be true and that every putt will drop. It means that you are finished with the basics and are ready for the next level of experiencing the game. You are ready to play golf!

If you wish, you may want to refer to our *Goal Setting Process* located on page 157. If you follow it precisely, you cannot fail. Use the *Goal Setting Process* now to learn the mechanics, or later to facilitate whatever you wish to accomplish (be it golf-related or not).

CHAPTER 9 WORDS TO FORGET

Do not believe them,
no matter what they say.

SWING
PLANE

Words are to the brain what keys are to a computer. Computers have in their memory different meanings for the same key. Nearly every manufacturer of computers makes the same basic keyboard. But nearly every software manufacturer has a totally different meaning stored in the chip even though the same key is pressed on the keyboard. Your brain is the same. Your concept of a word may be different than nearly everyone else's.

Blue! What color of blue did you see? Mine was turquoise. Was yours navy blue, sky blue, royal blue, or some other blue? Any ten people might have just as many answers.

This becomes a horrendous problem in learning golf when one instructor (amateur or professional) has a concept-meaning in his brain that's different than the concept-meaning in your brain. Talk about a serious communication problem and source of confusion!

For example, the pure-minded, uneducated in golf terminology can have a completely different understanding of the following terms than would the experienced player or professional.

TERM	Meaning to the pure-minded	Meaning to the golf pro
FORE	Number following three.	Duck! Here comes the ball.
ON A ROPE	A tight-rope walker.	A straight shot.
ONE DOWN	A beverage consumed.	One hole behind in a contest.
PLANE	Travel device.	Path of clubhead.

36

STRAIGHT	A backswing path that is straight.	A backswing path, diagonally slanting straight back and revolving inside the target line on a pre-described plane.
DOWN	Down (the direction).	Forward.
FINISH	Done.	The final position in the swing.
PAR	Average.	What the pro expects to score on a hole.

And it goes on. You can go nuts and look like a fool (which will motivate anyone to give up) if you are not discretionary as you listen to instructional terminology. You have two choices:

Choice 1: Forget those confusing terms. Do what you see, not what you hear. Make your own sense and use your own terminology that accurately describes your perception of the activity or instruction.

Choice 2: Listen to the terms. Then make sure that your concept and understanding of each matches exactly and precisely with the concept and understanding of that of an *expert* professional instructor.

Loaded words.

Be aware (beware) of the following. All these words can be regressive instead of progressive to your golf development.

GRIP	HIT
BACK	UP
PIVOT	DOWN
STILL (hold still)	STRAIGHT
CENTER (of swing)	HEAD DOWN
FAST	EYE ON BALL
SLOW	PLANE
HARD	PATH
EASY	STRONG
STANCE	WEAK
SWAY	TOP

Either forget all the above and stay ignorant (*ignore*-ant) or learn every meaning and variation in complete detail. Somewhere—anywhere—in the middle lies disaster.   37

CHAPTER 10
A CONTRACT

Sign this before going on.

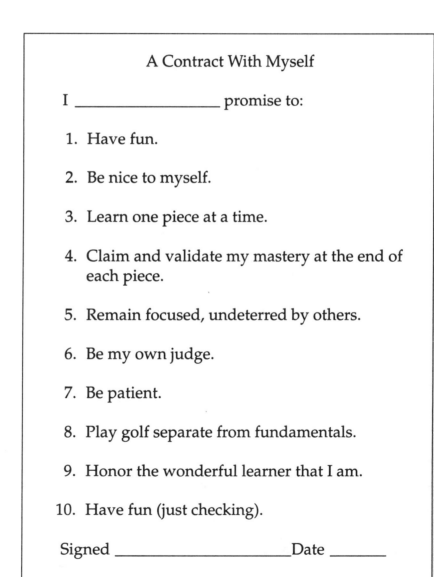

A Contract With Myself

I _____ promise to:

1. Have fun.

2. Be nice to myself.

3. Learn one piece at a time.

4. Claim and validate my mastery at the end of each piece.

5. Remain focused, undeterred by others.

6. Be my own judge.

7. Be patient.

8. Play golf separate from fundamentals.

9. Honor the wonderful learner that I am.

10. Have fun (just checking).

Signed _____ Date _____

CHAPTER 11
THE
FUN•DA•MENTALS
One piece at a time.

Before we get started on the job of learning the mechanical components of golf, understand the intent behind the presentation:

1.   Each piece (chunk of learning) is placed in sequential steps, first to last.

2.   Each piece is explained for your intellectual consumption.

3.   Each piece is given its own exercise so you will concretely experience the pieces in your sensory modes.

4.   Each piece has a way for you to know when you have accomplished learning it, so that you know when to claim your accomplishment of the skill, validate, graduate, and commence on learning the next piece.

Validation procedure.

   In conjunction with either the 3-STEP or 21-DAY learning methods, one more must be followed for the learning to "stick."

   We discussed the importance of graduating from a chunk of learning and claiming its mastery to be your own. Following is the most effective means to formalize this formality!

   Repeat the confirmation and affirmation suggested at the conclusion of each instructional chunk that is to follow this chapter. When you do so, look to six different positions, restating the message at each point. Speak the message first with your eyes directed to the lower left. Keep your head erect and still; move *only* your eyes. Next, look to the upper left, then upper middle, upper right, lower right, and, last, lower middle. It is very important to follow this validation procedure at the conclusion of each chunk of mechanics (otherwise, it may not be concluded!).

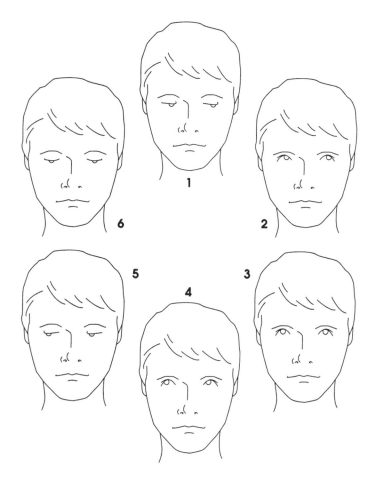

We could go into the "scientific" reasons this procedure aids retention, but let's suffice it to say that looking toward these six different directions as you repeat your confirmation and affirmation generates congruency between your conscious and subconscious minds. That's perfect.

Note: Not all the chapters that follow are accompanied by a suggested confirmation/affirmation statement, nor do they all have a suggested validation. *But each piece of learning still should be validated.* Some of the things you'll learn will be understood in such a subjective, unique manner that we cannot presuppose a specific validation procedure to affirm your mastery of every golfing skill. This is correct and possible with other mechanics that are somewhat less flexible: the grip, stance, and full swing, for instances. But the "final" forms of your putting, chipping, and wedge play, for other instances, are derived solely through your experiments. That is the only way you will find what works for you. Likewise, you must determine the specific validation and affirmations that give your way meaning to you.

The thing is: still do it!

There are two "sides" to golf—mechanical and non-mechanical. All the mechanics, or technique, of golf must be learned one at a time. Playing the game of golf is, in the interim, put on hold. BUT—not entirely! While you're learning the mechanics of the short game, you're also learning about playing golf. By the time you're through with all the things on the left, your experience with those on the right will merge seamlessly to make you a player of the game!

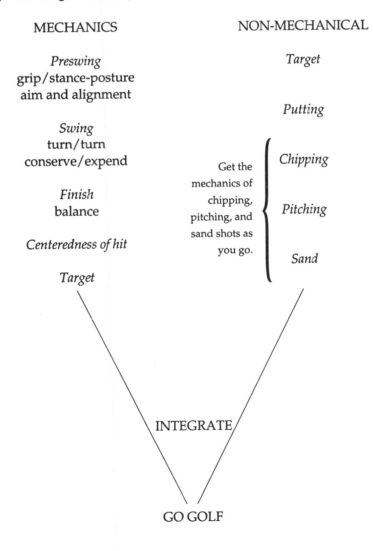

MECHANICS   NON-MECHANICAL

Preswing
grip/stance-posture
aim and alignment

Target

Putting

Swing
turn/turn
conserve/expend

Get the
mechanics of
chipping,
pitching, and
sand shots as
you go.

Chipping

Finish
balance

Pitching

Centeredness of hit

Sand

Target

INTEGRATE

GO GOLF

CHAPTER 12
MECHANICS

(aka: Fun-da-mentals. *Make them fun and mental and they will be easily physical!)*

Remember, you're going to follow either the 21-DAY or 3-STEP learning method to install each of the mechanics presented in this chapter. At this time, please review the preceding chapters that detail each method. Make sure the method you choose is itself clear and precise. If it's not, your use of either method will not produce precise results.

Hold on to your golf club—here we go!

CHAPTER 12.a.1
THE
NON-MOVING
PARTS

Hands position.

Your hand position on the golf club has always been called the "grip."

"Grip" is a misleading name because it can imply gripping or holding tightly. Actually, the (golf) grip is your sensitive, artistic connection to the golf club. In Australia it is called a "hold." Good idea!

By itself, your hand positioning is, by far, the most important component of the fundamentals. There is no such thing as a *pretty good* grip. It's either functional or nonfunctional.

Sorry that this part is arduous, but the grip is as important as all the rest put together.

STEP 1. Hold the club with the right hand so that the clubshaft is at 45-degree angle to the ground.

This is an important angle which automatically places the clubhandle in the proper position for the left hand.

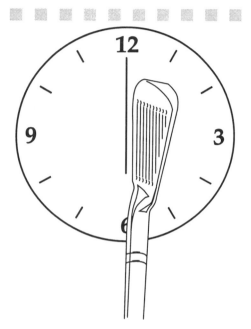

STEP 2. Turn the clubface so that its *leading* edge (lower edge, not top edge) is aligned to 12 o'clock (12:15 is an error preferable to 11:59).

STEP 3. Place the left hand on the clubhandle (reach to it as if you were shaking hands). About 1/4 to 1/2 inches of the butt of the clubhandle will extend beyond your hand.

Notice that the clubhandle is not completely in the palm of the hand; the handle runs across the second joint of the index finger.

44

OR *do this alternative:*

STEP 1a. Sole the club flat on the ground, clubhandle adjacent to the left hip.

STEP 2a. Grasp the clubhandle with your left hand and bring the club up to a 45-degree angle.

STEP 3a. Support it with your right hand. Align the leading edge to 12 o'clock.

NOTE: Steps 1a through 3a are to be used in lieu of Steps 1 through 3. Try both ways and use the one you feel gives the most consistent results.

Following either set of steps—1, 2, 3 or 1a, 2a, 3a—then takes you to Step 4 below.

STEP 4. The left hand position.
Maintain the leading edge at 12 o'clock with your right hand. Form a "V" shape between the thumb and forefinger (make sure it is not a "U" or "C" shape).

Notice that the club han- dle is directly under the thumb knuckle (not to one side of the thumb).

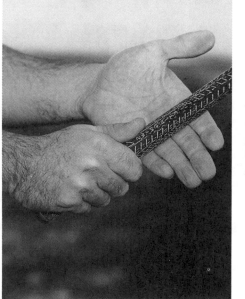

46

STEP 5. The right hand position.

First, identify the middle joints of the fingers (as opposed to the palm joints).

A. Slide the right hand to the left hand, palm up, so that the clubhandle lies across the middle joints. The two hands are not in contact.

B. Very slowly and precisely now, curl the fingers of the right hand.

C. Even more slowly and precisely, lay (don't wrap) the right hand directly down onto the left thumb. The meaty pad of the right hand thumb section is now on top of the left thumb.

Note: you will feel your right elbow drop down, toward your hip, as you lay your right hand *down* on your left thumb.

D. Touch your thumb to your forefinger so there is very slight contact of finger to thumb. This contact is slight —do not pinch the clubhandle!

This will form another "V" shape on the right hand.

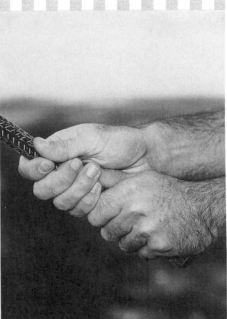

47

▨ STEP 6. Both hands.

A. Maintain the leading edge of the clubface at 12 o'clock.

B. Loosen the left hand on the club and rotate the left forearm in a clockwise direction until the left hand "V" points to your right shoulder.

C. Lighten your right hand pressure. Rotate your right hand counter-clockwise until the V points over your right shoulder, exactly parallel to the left hand V.

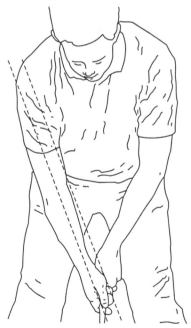

NOTE: The above two steps can be taken either with the club held up or placed on the ground. Most people find it easier and more accurate to sole the club before "tuning" the Vs.

48

D. The woman golfer with small to average size hands, and the junior golfer, has completed the hand position and has a "10-finger" grip. (photos on right)

The woman with large, strong hands, and most men golfers, can enhance the hand unity with an "overlapping" position (also called a "Vardon" grip). Lift the little finger of the right hand, slide the right hand snugly to the left and let the little finger overlap on top of the index finger of the left hand. (shown above left)

E. Finally, make sure that the leading edge of the clubface remains at 12 o'clock.

49

FINALLY! You're done with hand positioning mechanics!

Arduous? Maybe, but it must be precise, and, therefore, done with exacting, unwavering precision!

The hands position is as important as all other mechanics combined. Your hands—*and only your hands*—are responsible for the direction of the clubface throughout the golf swing and during the strike of the ball. And the direction of the clubface has the greatest influence in why the ball goes where it goes.

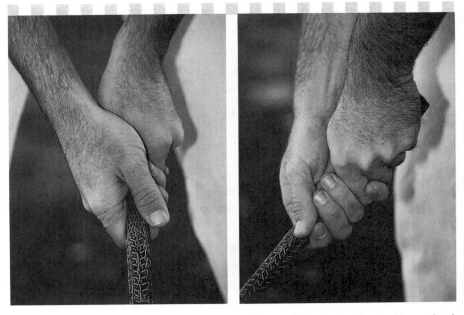

Here's what you end up with. The grip is the most "technical"—and important component of mechanics. Get it right and the rest is easy. Get it wrong, or don't get it consistently right, and the rest will be for naught. Among other things, the grip maintains clubface alignment during the swing.

Exercises for mastery of the grip.

Following is a unique set of exercises designed expressly and specifically for learning the hands position. What follows is neither the 3-STEP or 21-DAY learning method, but a "combination," of sorts, of each. Following these exercises is not a substitute for using either learning method, but is, instead, a vital supplement and first step to mastering hands position. More than that: it is a prerequisite. Stay with it; do not deviate. There is no more important fundamental and, unlike most other components of golfing mechanics, the hands position leaves very, very little room for personal interpretation. There is, in essence, one correct way to hold the club and countless incorrect ways.

You'll get the most benefit from these exercises if they are done daily for whatever period of time is required for you to recognize and confirm mastery.

EXERCISE 1

Sit in a chair. Take your hands on and off the club. Go very slowly and very precisely. Go through each step with absolute accuracy. Continue until each step is clearly and accurately established in your mind and is evidenced in your hand position and leading edge position. Go at your own rate for 10, 20, 30, 40 or more repetitions until you are completely satisfied that each step is unforgettable and accurate. Make sure that each position matches exactly with the model.

EXERCISE 2

Close your eyes. Form a mental picture of each step. Put your hands on the club as you process the picture in your mind. Open your eyes. Check your hand position for accuracy. Make any necessary adjustments in order to position your hands perfectly. Close your eyes and clarify your picture. Open your eyes to verify that what you see internally matches exactly with what your hands look like externally. Close your eyes. Form the perfect picture of your hand position. Add color to the picture. Make the picture bigger, brighter, clearer, more vivid and detailed. Keep adjusting and playing with the picture until you have unmistakable verification that you understand your hand position totally and completely.

EXERCISE 3

Standing or sitting, place the club into your perfect hand position. Close your eyes. Feel your hands relaxing, warming, and your blood flowing through your hands until you can feel the pulse in your fingertips. Imagine your hands melting together and merging with the golf club. Feel your hands increasing their sensitivity and connection with the club. You can barely, if at all, distinguish the difference between club and hands. Rotate your hands slowly to the right and then to the left. Feel the club and clubface rotating in unison with your hands. Imagine the leading edge at 10 o'clock, 1:30, 11:00 and 10:30. Imagine the direction the ball will travel when struck in any of these positions. Absorb the reference completely and fully. Imagine the artistry of it all. You are the artist. Thank yourself.

51

Validate and graduate.

As you follow the steps and exercises precisely, you will find that you quickly gain confidence and mastery. You will, within minutes or hours, find that, for example, your hands position on the club is "automatically" perfect and that you have a bonding with the club. You will know that you are at the mastery level when there are no "glitches."

Glitches occur when your internal picture is not "just right." It may lack color, detail, or clarity. The glitch may be in how the club feels. It may feel foreign or adversarial.

If "glitches" occur they are not a sign of "bad." They are simply a signal to continue the steps and exercises. Soon the glitches will disappear as your intuition signals your completion and supreme confidence in this element of the fundamentals. When you arrive at that moment, fill out the following statement of graduation.

Mastery of the hands position.
(Using the 3-STEP method.)

Here we go again! Yes indeed, this is getting repetitious. However, there is no more important fundamental than learning and habituating hands position mechanics. Repetition is the key to this critical chunk of learning. The three exercises presented for mastery of the hands position are uniquely designed to learn this critical skill.

Regardless of which learning method—21-DAY or 3-STEP—you choose to learn the other fundamental skills, follow the three hands position exercises outlined to their conclusion (habituation). After you've habituated the hands position using these three exercises, then proceed to using the 3-STEP method—if that's what you chose to learn the other skills. You do this for greater and deeper habituation of the hands position skill, and to keep consistent with employing the 3-STEP method in other skills learning.

So, onto the 3-STEP method. First, you need a model. The model can be the pictures in this text or a golfer that exemplifies the correct hands position.

You also need a mirror and a snapshot or videotape of yourself so that you can verify that what you are doing, in fact, matches the model of excellence that you want to achieve.

STEP 1. *See the model.* Close your eyes and see the model internally. Open your eyes and see the model externally. Close your eyes and adjust your internal picture until it matches perfectly with the external model. Do not attempt to feel anything; you will be in a disassociated state during these first two steps. You're on the outside looking in. Just get the picture perfectly adjusted and make sure there are no glitches in it.

STEP 2. *See yourself as the model.* Everything else is exactly the same except the picture that you see internally has your face, physique, and clothes. Keep seeing this internal picture until there are no glitches. Do not feel; remain disassociated.

STEP 3. *Become the model.* Associate! Step into the picture. Now you're on the inside looking out. Feel your hands on the clubhandle in perfect placement and union. Sense the perfect balance between the relaxed, supple touch of your hands and the control you have on the club and alignment of the clubface. Your hands, clubhandle, and clubface are in perfect, complementary unison. Feel this until there are no glitches.

Validation procedure.

Keep your head steady. Shift only your eyes to position one, lower left. Aloud, in a convincing voice, repeat the following statement in all six eye positions. Repeat again in all six positions.

I am becoming a competent and confident golfer. My hand position is fundamentally perfect. My hands are bonded mechanically perfect with the club. My hands are relaxed and sensitive with every motion of the clubface.

Diploma

I have completed the hand position on the club.
I have mastery of this portion, both mechanically and intuitively.
While I may wish to review the hand position at some future date(s),
it will be to confirm mastery of a sensitive and accurate hold.

Signed_____Date _____

CHAPTER 12.a.2
THE READY
POSITION
Address the ball: "Hello ball."

The "address" position is the name given to the *ready position* that you assume as you are about to hit the ball. Compared to the grip, this is simple, easy, and not nearly as precise.

■ Step 1. Stand tall, feet spread about shoulder-width (narrower is better than wider).

Step 2. Flex your knees. There is not a big bend in the knees, just enough flex to provide mobility.

Step 3. Tilt your spine forward from your hips—it is *not* a bend from the waist. There is no rounding of the shoulders or bowing of the spine.

Tilt forward (from the hips) until your arm simply hangs *vertically* and the club soles flat on the ground.

You might try the following exercise to get the sensation of the spine tilting instead of bending:

Standing erect, measure the distance from your chin to your chest with the thumb and little finger of your right hand. Now tilt forward at the hips until you can see the ball without diminishing the distance from chin to chest. Note the line drawn to illustrate this measurement.

55

Step 4. The ready position is a ready-to-go position. You should feel light and mobile on your feet as if you were ready to run, dance, or spring into the air. It's the sensation that you have after having just stepped on your dance partner's toes... Feel very light on the ground, almost floating.

DO NOT dig in or get heavy. Be a ballerina, not a nose-tackle.

That's it! It's very simple, very easy. All you need to do is to get in the same ready position each time you prepare to play a shot.

56

NOTE: As the clubs increase in length, you will automatically move farther and farther from the ball. But the address position is still the same! Study these two pictures and note that while one is with the longest club (driver) and the other is with the shortest club (a wedge), the posture and arms hang is the same.

(The only other difference is that the stance gets a little wider as the clubs get longer. This is a naturally-occurring adjustment that will be made purely through your sense of balance.)

57

Mastery of the ready position. (Using the 3-STEP method.)

Find a model. The model can be the pictures in this text or a golfer that exemplifies the correct ready position posture.

You also need a mirror and a snapshot or videotape of yourself so that you can verify that what you are doing, in fact, matches the model of excellence that you want to achieve.

STEP 1. *See the model.* Close your eyes and see the model internally. Open your eyes and see the model externally. Close your eyes and adjust your internal picture until it matches perfectly with the external model. Do not attempt to feel anything; you will be in a disassociated state during these first two steps. You're on the outside looking in. Just get the picture perfectly adjusted and make sure there are no glitches in it.

STEP 2. *See yourself as the model.* Everything else is exactly the same except the picture that you see internally has your face, physique, and clothes. Keep seeing this internal picture until there are no glitches. Do not feel; remain disassociated.

STEP 3. *Become the model.* Associate! Step into the picture. Now you're on the inside looking out. Feel your knee flex, spine tilt, arms hanging comfortably, and especially the lightness and mobility of your feet. Feel the poise and readiness of your body. Feel your body ready to move with agility, suppleness, grace, and perfect balance. Feel this until there are no glitches.

Validation procedure.

In each of the six eye positions, repeat the following statement aloud in a convincing voice. Repeat one more time in all six positions.

I am becoming a competent and confident golfer. My ready position is perfectly functional. My knees are flexed, my spine is tilted so my arms hang freely. I am mobile and balanced on my feet.

Diploma

I have the perfect ready position for me.
My knees are flexed.
My arms hang comfortably from my shoulders.
My spine is straight and tilts from my hips.
I am ready for graceful and balanced motion.
I have mastered the ready position.

Signed_____Date _____

CHAPTER 12.a.3 AIMING PROCEDURE

Setting up for success.

Mastery of the non-moving parts precedes learning the moving parts used in hitting the ball.

So, after you have mastered the mechanics of hand position and ready position, now get ready for the GO! Get comfortable to make motion—the swing—without hesitation.

Exercise: Place a ball on the ground, floor, or grass. Pick a target, any target. Pick something at which you can aim: a spot on the wall, a telephone pole, the dog, or anything you wish.

■ Practice a three-step procedure:
Step 1. Put your hands on the club
in perfect position.

Step 2. Walk to the ball, aim at your target, and then assume your ready position.

Step 3. Without hesitation, feel yourself *activate*—get ready to swing. This feeling of activating may be a bodily sensation such as being aware of the lightness of your feet, or it may be an internal image of the target—whatever gives you the sense that you are ready to go!

Imitate the actions of a competent, decisive professional.

61

Aiming Procedure.

Aim, then align.
　　Aim = clubface.
　　Align = body (feet, knees, hips, and shoulders).

Step 1. After having placed your hands in perfect position on the clubhandle, approach the golf ball from behind it, looking toward the target. As you do this, imagine one line going straight to the target and another perpendicular line bisecting the golf ball.

Step 2. Always set and aim the clubface *first* by placing it down behind the ball with the clubface at 90-degrees to the target line. Aim the clubface before any part of your body crosses to the target-side of the perpendicular line.

Step 3. When the clubface is aimed and set, then *align* your body-lines at 90-degrees to the perpendicular line (clubface) and parallel to the target line. Your feet, knees, hips, and shoulders are all *square*—parallel to the target line.

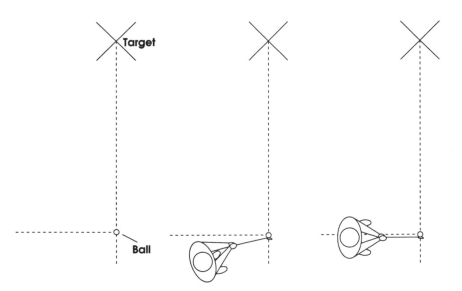

Note: This procedure is not used by most golfers, but it is correct, and, there-fore, is the way *you* should set up to the ball. Following this method will eliminate the mis-aiming found in the procedure used by the "old" model (addressing the ball *before* aiming or aligning). You will simply be "way ahead of the game" by aiming first and aligning second. You'll avoid the potential for distortion of aim and alignment by your visual system. Enough said, but the aiming procedure is very, very important to proficient golf.

Aim the clubface, not your feet, at the target. Since you are standing away from the ball, your stance line will be to a point parallel-left of the target line. Also note that other body parts stay on this parallel-left line: feet, knees, hips, arms, shoulders.

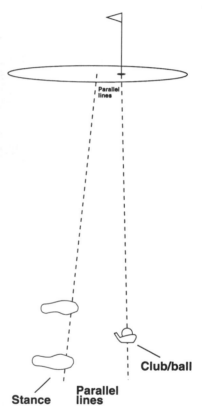

Note, too: You'll hear the terms "open" and "closed" associated with the alignment of the feet.

When they refer to the stance line, these terms mean just the opposite of what they do when they refer to the clubface. In the stance, open means facing left of the target and closed means facing right of the target. Ignore all this and stand square —parallel—to the target.

63

CHAPTER 12.b
THE
MOVING
PARTS
(aka the golf swing)

The swing is easy! It's as simple as:

> *Around.*
> *And around again.*
> *A "swish" in the middle.*
> *And stand up at the end.*

If someone accuses you of swinging like a baseball batter, say "thank you." The golf swing you will learn is as simple as a baseball swing, except that the ball you'll hit isn't moving.

Consider the ready position for a baseball swing. It's very much that of the golfing ready position with two exceptions:

1. In baseball, your target (the ball) is higher, so the plane of the swing will be more parallel to the ground.

2. And your arms are more horizontal instead of hanging downward.

The baseball swing is an around-and-around motion of your semi-vertical spine.

The golf swing is a motion around-and-around your tilted spine.

Close your eyes. Visualize the baseball batter's motion, especially the forward swing at a stomach-high ball. Imagine the circular motion and arc of the arms and bat. Imagine the turning motion of the body as it generates the swing of the arms and bat.

Sense the rhythm and balance of the motion, smooth and powerful.

Feel the turn of your body, the swing of your arms, and the mobility in your feet.

Open your eyes and reflect upon this experience. Repeat the exercise until you can "see" the picture in a clear, precise manner and can feel the activity as you see it.

▨ Then close your eyes again. Visualize this baseball player in the golfer's ready position, and with a golf club instead of a bat. Imagine the same motion of turning and swinging except at the tilted arc appropriate for striking a golf ball.

Sense the wonderfully balanced and rhythmic motion of your turn and swing as it is generated from your feet. Your body turns with the grace of a dancer, your arms are moving in perfect cadence with your body. Hear the club swish through the air as it accumulates speed.

Feel the sensation of light, sensitive hands. Your wrists are fluid and supple. Your balance is impeccable. Continue this exercise. As you repeat the exercise, you will experience increased vividness in your internal picture, not unlike tuning your television to become brighter, clearer, and more detailed. You will also sense bodily feelings such as the mobility of your feet, the grace of your turning motion, the fluidness of your arms, the relaxation in your hands, and the overall performance of your motor skills and athleticism.

NOTE: The finish position is not shown in these photos (there will be *a lot* more said about this vital position). For comparison's sake, the position illustrated in the third photos shows very clearly the relationship between baseball and golf with respect to how clubface aim follows swing plane. But when you practice this, by all means finish your swings!

67

The swing begins at the end.

It is the balanced position which you achieve at the end of your motion that measures the quality of your swing from beginning to end. The most simple, easiest way to master a great swing is to master a great finish position.

The finish position is easily mastered by allowing your feet to be light, mobile, and rhythmic through your swing. The killer of motion and mobility is flat, heavy, immobile feet. If you don't believe that, then all you have to do is attempt dancing with your feet flat and heavy. Good luck!

The finish position is easy if you imagine yourself to be a ballet dancer. Your swing simply begins with your left knee, hip and shoulder turning clockwise, arms and club following in unison until you are comfortably coiled.

The dancer in you then reverses the turn, legs leading the way back. The arms and club "swish" through.

Your turning motion toward your intended target is powerful yet graceful and rhythmic as monitored by the sensations of motion and balance in your feet.

The motion completes itself as you turn to face your intended target, following naturally the centrifugal force of your club and arms. Your finish position is the logical completion of your motion and balance. It is the statement of your swing efficiency.

You will be supported on your left foot. Your right toe simply balances you. There is essentially no weight on your right toe or foot. Your turning motion is complete as indicated by your right knee pointed at your target, your chest fac-

68

ing your target. The club and arms will complete their motion. Your arms are relaxed. The club is either behind your head or behind and slightly over your head. Your head is erect and your eyes are tracking the ball as it arcs gracefully, accelerating away and soaring toward your target.

This is the perfect finish of motion that will make you look like a golfer and play like a player.

EXERCISE 1

You don't need a club to practice this position. Simply assume the ready position. Pretend that your left thumb is the clubshaft. Hold on to your left thumb with your right hand. Turn to the finish position. Hold the finish position. Maintain your balance and posture.

Close your eyes. Feel your balance, the distribution of weight to your left foot. Feel your right toe simply as a balancing point. Feel your right knee and chest facing your target. Feel your arms, relaxed and comfortable. Maintain the position for thirty to sixty seconds. Sense the balance and grace of your mind and body. You can amplify the sense of athleticism as you imagine that your finish position is every bit as attractive and efficient as any great golfer's.

▓ EXERCISE 2 ▓

Repeat Exercise 1 except now use a golf club. Turn back, away from the target. Feel your motion, rhythm and balance. Turn to a comfortable coil. Conserve energy.

Turn toward the target by activating the return motion in your feet and legs, expending energy in grace and power. Feel your arms and clubhead generating speed following the lead of your legs and hips. Hear the club "swish" through the air.

Follow your clubhead to a totally balanced finish.

Hold your finish. Close your eyes and feel your balance and completion. Adjust any elements of the position to fit the model. Then embellish your finish position by relishing in your sensations through your feet, legs, trunk, arms, and hands.

Repeat Exercises 1 and 2 until your finish position is the completion of every swing you make. Your mastery of the finish position will generate the best golf swing that you can make. The thousand pieces of advice and suggestions that you will receive regarding your swing will be eliminated as you master the perfect finish to your swing.

A couple of details.

Unfortunately, the word "straight" and the concepts associated with "straight" can tie golfers into knots.

A "straight" clubface is a relative term when considered in conjunction with a diagonal swing plane and a turning body motion. You can eliminate confusion and difficulty by internalizing the following motor skills.

You can also eliminate the confusion by perfecting your hands position! Remember, it is your "grip" that determines, more than anything else, how well you maintain a "straight" clubface.

Take an in-depth look at a golfer standing erect, like the baseball batter. Hands are in front of the chest, clubshaft is horizontal, the clubface is aimed "straight" at the target. At the completion of the coiling turn away from the target, the clubface should point "straight" at the sky to be "straight" at the target.

Study the above picture carefully. Then practice this activity until you achieve this position comfortably and naturally. The key is *comfortably* and *naturally*. Proceed only after this is comfortable and natural.

Swing forward, starting the motion with your feet, legs, and hips. Simply be active in your lower body as you are when dancing.

At the finish of the spine-upright swing, the clubface will point "straight" at the ground; it will be an exact mirror-image of the above photo. This finish position is exactly the same as the golf swing (tilted spine) except that your arms and clubshaft are finishing below the level of your shoulders. Practice this position until it is *comfortable* and *natural*. Then, combine the away-turn with the forward-turn until you match the model *comfortably* and *naturally*.

DO NOT proceed to the golf swing (tilted spine) until you are totally precise, comfortable, and natural with the "horizontal" swing. Confirm your mastery in a mirror, video playback, and/or with those hundreds of admiring spectators looking on!

Now, tilt your spine, assume the golfing ready position, and make the same motion on the golfer's tilted plane.

Your motion should feel the same, especially in your relaxed hands and arms. At waist-high, the toe of the club will point up in the away-turn and up again at

73

waist-high in the forward-turn. All else will occur *naturally* and *comfortably* as you swing to your perfect finish position.

The clubface will deliver the ball to exactly where you aim.

REVIEW OF THE SWING

- A proficient swing is easy after an efficient hands position and ready position are mastered.

- The swing is as easy as around-and-around and stand up at the end.

- A perfect finish position indicates a perfect swing, and, therefore, is the perfect way to learn the perfect swing.

- Your feet, legs, and hips must be active and rhythmic to produce an easy, proficient swing.

74

- A "straight" clubface is "straight up" and "straight down" when you swing with your spine vertical. Straight is "toe up, toe up" when you make a spine-tilted golf swing.

Note: All this "study" of motion will be infinitely easier and more natural if you simply swing to music. Listen to music via the radio, stereo, boom-box, or headset. The rhythm and balance will be easy and natural. *Around and around, around and around...* What music have you heard that has this two-beat rhythm?

You may also wish to visualize a metronome moving rhythmically back and forth—*around and around.*

Mastery of the golf swing.
(Using the 3-STEP method.)

STEP 1. SEE the model. With your eyes open or closed, view your swing model with perfect clarity until you only see this picture any time you think of the golf swing.

STEP 2. SEE yourself as the model. Keep viewing yourself until you swing as the model does. See yourself from the outside by viewing your swing in a mirror or video playback. With your eyes closed you will see your own face and swing. Continue this process until there are no glitches. Your swing appears to you the same every time: eyes open or closed. *Do not feel,* just see.

STEP 3. FEEL your swing from the inside. Feel your motion, turn, mobility, cadence, relaxation, rhythm, balance, coiling, conserving. Feel your forward turn, arms and club accelerating, expending energy and power. Feel your finish position and perfect balance. Feel until there are no glitches. Feel your empowerment, athletics, esteem, and confidence. Say YES, and smile accordingly.

Remember: At any time you become confused or disorganized regarding your golf swing, simply return to the vertical-spine swing and recapture your sense of confidence.

Validation procedure.
  In each of the six positions, repeat the following aloud:
  I am the master of the golf swing.
  I finish every swing in perfect balance.

Diploma

I am the master of the golf swing.
I finish every swing on perfect balance.

Signed_____Date _____

CHAPTER 12.c
NOW THE BALL
Ah, the blessed ball.

Isn't that interesting...

Until now there hasn't been much mention of the ball. The striking of the ball is an entirely separate task requiring an entirely different focus than anything you've learned up to this point.

Had you interjected the ball prematurely, you may have overlooked all previous skill-building in order to "hit" the ball.

The trick is to build the pre-swing and swing skills first. Then those skills will not be sacrificed when the ball is introduced.

Striking the ball is simply a matter of focusing your mind on the center of the clubface striking the center of the back of the ball. This does not imply tension or manipulation on your part. It simply is a matter of focusing your mind—your inner eye—on the club-ball relationship.

You cannot fail.

You might swing over the top of the ball or hit the top of the ball. This is your opportunity to realize that the clubface is too high and adjust

accordingly. The same is true should you hit low behind the ball.

Stay relaxed. Allow your swing to flow freely and finish in balance. Make your adjustments with your focus. Acknowledge and verify the solid, centered strikes. They will come faster and easier.

This is a critical period in your development. You may find yourself feeling stranded, vulnerable to advice from every Tom, Dick, and Harriet. Let it be. Then return to a relaxed and comfortable athletic ready position, focus, swing, and let the centered strike occur.

Centeredness of contact.

You appreciate that the center of your clubface is designed to make contact with the center of the ball during your forward swing. There is no conflict in this concept, only harmony.

You can more fully imprint this compatibility and harmony into your mind by doing the following exercise.

79

EXERCISE

SEE the ball on the center of your clubface. Simply place the ball on the face of the club. Center it on the clubface.

Close your eyes and maintain the visual image of the ball on the center of the clubface.

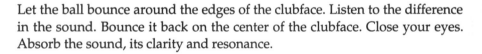

Now imagine the ball on the ground, the clubhead moving toward the ball on its forward motion. See the ball and clubface coming together, center to center.

In your mind, see the centeredness of contact from various angles: above, below, behind, and from the heel of the club. Embellish the center of the clubface and back of the ball with color or designs.

HEAR the centeredness of contact. Bounce the ball on the center of the clubface. Listen to the sound of the ball and club as they make contact.

Let the ball bounce around the edges of the clubface. Listen to the difference in the sound. Bounce it back on the center of the clubface. Close your eyes. Absorb the sound, its clarity and resonance.

FEEL the difference that is apparent between centered and off-centered bounces. Notice how solid and steady the centered contact is compared to the off-centered contact. Close your eyes. Absorb the feel of the centered hit. Distinguish the difference in feelings.

With these sensory references clearly established, you will quickly find the centeredness of contact as you make your swing to and through the ball.

Now approach the ball. Maintain your perfect grip and ready position. By moving your feet, adjust your distance from the ball so that the ball is

80

centered in the clubface, the clubhead soled flat on the ground.

The ball will be centered between your feet for irons and more toward your left foot for woods.

Two small suggestions.

1.   If you find yourself repeatedly swinging too high relative to the ball, then you are probably setting up to the ball in a "reaching" position. Stand closer to the ball and let your arms relax.

2.   If you are repeatedly hitting the ground behind the ball before striking the ball itself, then you are probably crowding in too close to the ball. Back off just an inch or two.

Note: Nobody means to give the advice "keep your head down" or "keep your eye on the ball." These are inaccurate and imprecise commands. The intent of the advice is to have you focus your mind on the centeredness of hit. If, at any time, you are having difficulty achieving centeredness of hit, simply process through the preceding exercises for relief.

Also note that your success with centering the hit is very much dependent on the fit of your clubs. If your clubs don't fit you, the ball will not be stuck squarely or fly straight unless you compensate for the ill-fitted clubs by altering your swing. More about that next.

CHAPTER 12.d AND NOW THE CLUBS

Weapons of mass construction.

Before you jump into the playing of golf and hitting a lot of balls, there is one more, CRITICAL consideration: *golf clubs which fit you.*

No more than you would run a marathon in wrong-sized cowboy boots or type with garden gloves on, should you attempt to achieve centeredness of contact and satisfying

golf shots with misfit clubs. It's been said that a mechanic is only as good as his tools; your mechanics may likewise only be as good as *your* tools.

Without properly-fit clubs, you will be disadvantaged. Worse yet, you will believe that you are doing poorly when, in fact, much of the fault is in the equipment.

The club is a part of the cybernetic loop to your brain. The simple reality is that you must make too many physical compensations to achieve centered, powerful hits with a misfit piece of equipment.

These compensations can ruin your swing and remove the fun from golf.*

DANGER, DANGER, DANGER!

1. Do not purchase equipment that does not fit you (or that which cannot be made to fit you by a competent, professional clubfitter).

Used equipment is perfectly acceptable and is probably a wise choice—provided that it fits you.

2.   Women, do not use cast-aside men's equipment.

3.   Do not give heavy, cut-down, adult equipment to juniors.

(All the aforementioned equipment should be donated to your enemies or to friends with whom you will be making future golfing wagers.)

The rule of thumb is this: You are far better off with only a few properly-fit clubs than you are with a whole bag full of misfit clubs. Misfit clubs are far too expensive at any price, no matter how pretty they look or how convincing the salesperson may be.

At the time of this writing, I recommend the Henry-Griffiths® method of clubfitting. Regardless of which brand of clubs you may purchase, the Henry-Griffiths® fitting method appears to be the most accurate system available at this point in the evolution of equipment fitting.

You may reach their headquarters by calling 1-800-445-GOLF.

We'll talk more about clubs later in the book, but the three basics of a proper fit are 1) proper shaft flex and length, 2) proper grip diameter, 3) proper lie angle.

*An accomplished athlete can recalibrate neuro-muscular responses and appear to produce efficient shots with misfit equipment. In other words: an experienced golfer can make his or her swing fit the equipment. He or she will, however, never achieve potential until the equipment fits, activating his or her parasympathetic system.

CHAPTER 12.e FINALLY, THE TARGET

And now we have golf.

So far, you have separated the pieces of learning into their individual components: hand position, ready position, swing, and ball. You have progressed through each piece and validated your accomplishment of each. Pat yourself on the back. Your mind is prepared and clear. You are ready to introduce the target.

With the target as your objective, your awareness does not shift entirely to target awareness. To do so would make your activity a pure *reaction*. You would lose all sense of self and you may even "space-out." You will ultimately play golf as a blend of self-awareness and target-awareness in a cybernetic loop. Your activity will be dictated by the target and its conditions, of which you are one. Golf will become an *interaction*.

At that time, you will be the envy of all golfers, great and not-so-great,

regardless of the score you produce. You will be a true *player of the game*.

To reach this ultimate state requires a total indulgence in the play. Remember play? It is something we did as children before the days of "what will they think of me?"

As you play, in the truest sense of the word, the work of learning the nature of interaction will go on below your conscious awareness. The rise of *intelligence* will occur.

Intelligence is far different and far greater than *intellect*.

You used your intellect to "figure out" the pre-golf fundamentals. Now it is time to let go of intellect as you are interacting with the target during your swing. Your conscious mind will quiet. Your intelligent, subtle mind will synthesize millions of bits of information in your wondrous brain, activating your physical motion.

The ball will be struck or not be struck. The ball will go somewhere, accurate or inaccurate. In a true sense of play, absent of self-criticism or judgement, just go hit it again. The fact that your aim and intent to hit the ball to your target during the subsequent swing means, by definition, that you are discriminating. Hit the ball and hit it again. Play and play again. Enjoy yourself—there is nothing else to enjoy. Improvement in your proficiency will be forthcoming and recognized only in retrospect.

PLAYING is everything!

Choose to have fun.

Action yields results.

Fun creates enjoyment.

Knowledge facilitates action.

Enjoyment invites participation.

Insight generates knowledge.

Participation focuses attention.

Awareness promotes insight.

Attention expands awareness.

TARGET PROCESSING

1. Based on the conditions of the shot, distance to the target, lie of the ball, elevation of the target, wind direction and velocity, how you feel—and an infinite number of other target condition variables—you will pick the club that gives you the best opportunity to advance the ball to the most suitable position.

   Note: In the beginning, don't worry about which club you're hitting. You'll figure it out through PLAY. The shorter clubs propel the ball shorter and higher. The ball goes longer and lower with longer clubs. Just play. Enjoy the process of discovery.

2. From behind the ball, looking toward your target, take a practice swing appropriate for the shot. Rehearse the shot.

3. Take a deep, natural breath into your diaphragm. Relax. Focus on the target. Be decisive.

4. Without hesitation, now move to the ball. Ready yourself. Settle. Hit the ball.

5. Get excited when the ball flies to a position that's in functional proximity to your target. OR, in the case of undesirable outcomes, replay the shot in your mind as you would like the outcome to be. Get excited about the outcome of the replay.

6. Find the ball and hit it again.

7. Continue this practice until the ball is in the hole. That's golf.

Playing each shot requires a simple routine, and your undivided attention. The critical element is that your focus is away from self, meaning that you're not thinking about anything but getting the ball to the target. When you're on the course, there is no need, room, or time to focus on your swing, your clubs, or your score.

Take a practice swing that's appropriate for the shot you're about to play. Rehearse what you need to do.

Move to the ball, aim at the target, and assume your ready posture.

Relax and take a breath. Focus on the target.

87

Through experiments and experience (which should always be the same) you've discovered the sensations you have when you activate your body in preparation to play a shot. *Activate.*

88

Now swing through the ball!

Watch it fly wherever it may go. If it flies within a functional proximity of the target, get excited! If it doesn't, then visualize the way you wished it to fly and get excited about that.

No matter where the ball goes, go after it! Find the ball and hit it again. Keep on until the ball is in the hole. This wonderful pursuit is the GAME of golf!

89

THE LITTLE SHOTS

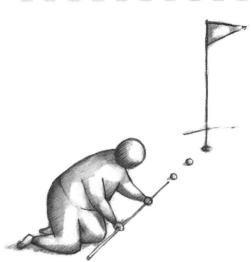

Most of your score, no matter what your level of play—professional to beginner—comes more from short shots than long shots. According to statistics we've kept on players of all abilities, the full shot, where you use the club for its full potential of distance, constitutes only 37-percent of your score. The other 63-percent of your score comes from putting, chipping, and pitching.

As golf shots become shorter, the need for accuracy becomes greater. The target is being successively reduced in size. The target was the fairway, then the green, then close proximity to the hole, and finally into the hole—a circle 4-1/2 inches in diameter.

The full swing is for fairway and green targets. The pitch and chip are for greens and close proximity to the hole. On these little shots, the ultimate reward is when the ball falls into the hole unexpectedly.

Note: Follow the aiming procedure for all short shots, including putts. That is to aim first (the clubface) and then align second (the body).

CHAPTER 12.f
THE REALLY LITTLE
SHOTS
aka: putting

Here is how to learn to putt:

Putt! Putt! Putt! Putt! Putt! Putt!
Putt! Putt! Putt! Putt! Putt! Putt!
Putt! Putt! Putt! Putt! Putt! Putt!

You teach yourself how to putt. There is no right or wrong way.

There is only *your way.*

It is in finding your best way to roll the ball into the hole where you have the ultimate opportunity to put your perfect learning powers to use.

So try every conceivable method, sensical or non-sensical.

Stand tall, short, closed, open, close to the ball, far-away from the ball.

Position the ball forward, middle, back.

Try a long putter, short putter, extra-long putter.

Try a blade putter, center-shafted, mallet, lined, unlined, heel-shafted, homemade.

Try a big grip, small grip, leather, rubber, textured, non-textured.

There may well be hundreds of different putter designs.

Try them all!

91

Putting will constitute 40-percent of your score, beginner or pro!

Anyone can master putting!

You can be a pro (plus) at 40-percent of the game!

You can have low scores!

Putting is easy. It's three steps:

1. Aim
2. Fire
3. Pick the ball out of the hole, or repeat Steps 1 and 2.

There are only two considerations that will be of real value:

1. Experiment until you find a putting method which enhances the accuracy of your visual perception of the target's location.

You'll know what that is when you discover that the ball is rolling along the path you want and is finishing up where you think it should nearly all the time (there will always be little inconsistencies in the putting surface and mistakes made in judgement than can cause a ball to go where you don't want it to).

2. Experiment until you find a putter that feels and looks right to you and further enhances your perceptual accuracy.

You'll know what that is when you find that you easily and accurately can sense the energy, alignment, and centeredness of contact on any and every putt you play.

Take your time—3, 6, 12, 18 months—whatever it takes. Then, once you have satisfied both factors, settle into a pre-shot routine or procedure for "reading" the putt (the method by which you look at the path to the hole and determine how the ball will roll along it), walking into your ready position, and then stroking the ball.

Then do not deviate, forever and ever, amen.

Putting is a matter of imagery. You can either imagine the ball going into the hole at the right speed and along the right path or you can't. You might imagine it through seeing, feeling, or sensing rhythm, or any combination in any personal order. The "trick" then is to putt. Practice and play at putting. Play and practice at putting. Take delight in the play, and the practice will go on unawares.

Play your partner or spouse for nickels, dollars, or for who does the dishes. Play at long putts, short putts, and in between putts. Play at sidehill, uphill, downhill putts.

Be a child. How many games can you invent? How many ways are there to be attracted, engaged, and entertained? Therein lies your ability to become a great putter. If you putt a lot you'll become okay at putting. But if putting is *play*, you'll become great. If putting is work—well, good luck. If you *play* putting for the fun of it, you will become great. If you practice putting because it will get you something or take you somewhere, then— good luck.

One more idea: Most people don't hold the putter the same as they do the other clubs. Since there's no need for a long, powerful swing, the hands should probably face one another so that both palms are perpendicular to the putter-face. This helps keep the putter-face straight. Also, many golfers use a "reverse" overlap grip. Instead of the right-hand little finger being over the left-hand index finger, the left-hand index finger is over the right-hand little finger. This gripping style is a good place to start your experiments.

Mastery of the putt.
(Using the 3-STEP method.)

STEP 1. SEE the model until your picture is perfectly adjusted and consistent.

STEP 2. SEE your face on the model until your picture is perfectly adjusted and consistent.

STEP 3. FEEL the stroke and distance. Repeat until you know you have "it." Then play, play, play in your practice to experience and develop the "feel" for the necessary amount of energy to get the ball to the proximity of the hole.

Validation procedure.
    Up to you! Just remember to do it.
    We mentioned earlier in Chapter 11 that we couldn't always supply you with the appropriate confirmation/affirmation statement. Here is a case in point. You will find that there are many, many ways you can get a ball into the hole. One will be best for you. When you determine which way that is, make it very clear to yourself and you'll easily create a statement that stands for the sensations you experience when you've "got it."

Diploma

I am the master of the putting stroke.
I...

Signed_____Date _____

CHAPTER 12.g
VERY LITTLE SHOTS
aka: chip shots

A chip shot might be played anywhere from very close to the hole to several yards away from the hole. A chip is like a putt with a hop in it.

For chipping, use a 6, 7, 8, or 9 iron, or one of your wedges.

Which club you use will depend on the rolling room there is after the ball lands on the green. The more rolling room, the less lofted (lower numbered) the club, and vice-versa.

Experiment to find what different clubs will produce for you when used from varying distances. You'll find that different-numbered irons will produce different proportions of "air-time" and roll. The lower lofted the club, the shorter the flight and the longer the run, and vice-versa.

Chipping accuracy increases when you can roll the ball along the ground *toward* the hole rather than fly the ball through the air *to* the hole. Since it demands such exacting accuracy, that is why putting is a rolling game. It is also why the chip shot should have just enough flight time to get the ball onto the green and roll it to the proximity of the hole. Refer to the diagram below to get a better idea of how this works. (You might also find one or two clubs you're confident with instead, and there's nothing wrong with using only those.)

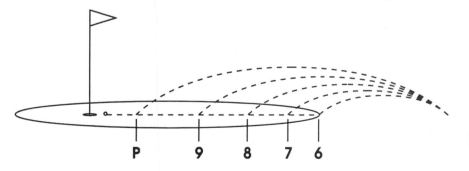

P   9   8   7   6

Fundamentally, there are a few changes in your mechanics to play a chip shot.

1. Stand *very* close to the ball. The ball is perhaps only 8-10 inches from your toes. The clubshaft will be abnormally vertical. While this will be much different than if you were using the club to hit a "full" shot, it's okay since we are not using it to play the full shot for which it was designed.

We are using it for accuracy so we are making a putter out of an iron, except that the loft on the club-face will get the ball elevated just long enough to fly the ball onto the green.

2. Keep the clubface pointing to the target. "Open" your body lines to the target line. This position will help enhance your visual fix on the target. The ball will appear to be located in front of your right toe.

3. Lean your whole body toward the target so that most of your weight is balanced on your left foot.

Your swing is very small because the distance is very short. During the stroke of the chip, your weight will remain on your left foot; it won't shift over and back as it does in a full swing. There will be very little or no body motion because there is such minimal energy needed to propel the ball an accurate distance. The only "rule" is conserve and expend. Your forward motion will always have more energy than your back motion.

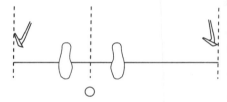

If you are *consistently* hitting the ball "thin" (above the ball's center-line) or "fat" (hitting the ground before hitting the ball), make sure your weight is on the left side and is *staying there* during the stroke.

97

Mastery of the chip shot.
(Using the 3-STEP method.)

STEP 1. SEE the model until your picture is perfectly adjusted and consistent.

STEP 2. SEE your face on the model until your picture is perfectly adjusted and consistent.

STEP 3. FEEL your motion and shot. Repeat until you know you have "it." Then play, play, play in your practice to experience and develop the "feel" for the necessary amount of energy to get the ball to the proximity of the hole.

Validation procedure.

Up to you! Just remember to do it. Same as for putting: there are too many "good" ways to hit a chip shot to encumber you with only one means to validate the way you discover.

Diploma

I am the master of the chipping stroke.
I...

Signed_____Date _____

CHAPTER 12.h
LITTLE SHOTS
aka: the pitch

The swing used to play a pitch shot is an abbreviation of the full swing.

Depending on your strength, and other factors, a full swing with a pitching club (pitching wedge or sand wedge, the shortest and most lofted clubs) may propel the ball 40-140 yards. The ball goes high in the air, descends steeply, lands softly, and rolls minimally.

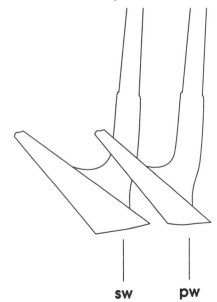

sw   pw

This chapter is concerned with using the pitching and sand wedges to produce shots that suit the distance necessary to get the ball to the target.

But first, the clubs.

The pitching wedge (PW) is almost identical to the 9-iron except that the pitching wedge has more loft. More loft means a higher, shorter flight and more backspin.

A sand wedge (SW) has a wider, heavier sole than a pitching wedge and yet even more loft. Also, if you'll sight along the bottom of most sand wedges you'll see that the trailing edge of the sole is lower than the leading edge. This is called "bounce," and is designed to help the club float through sand and taller grass without "digging in."

Now to their use.

Fundamentally, your ready position for a pitch is the same as for a full shot, except that:

1. You may want to narrow your stance as the shots get shorter.
2. You may want to stand closer to the ball as the shots get shorter.

If you are *consistently* hitting the ball "thin" (above the ball's centerline) move closer to the ball. If you are *consistently* hitting the ball "fat" (ground sooner than ball), then move away from the ball.

Just like throwing or kicking a ball, the motion is the same as for a long throw or kick. There is simply less of it.

The "less of it" is most emphatic on the backswing, *not* on the forward swing.

It is essential that you *conserve* energy when turning-coiling away from the target and *expend* energy toward the target, regardless of the distance of the shot to be hit. Impact with the ball is still "sharp." The sensation is one of the clubhead *accelerating* through the ball.

The key is to stay mobile on your feet. The rotation of your body, emphatically during the forward turn, will be active—as mobilized by your feet.

101

The same concept of energy expenditure is true for throwing or kicking a ball. You would conserve energy in your back-motion and expend energy in your forward-motion. To maintain control of distance (and accuracy), your follow-through would always be longer than your backswing.

The pitch shot is a small golf swing motion. There is less backswing than there is followthrough. You may use only a fraction of your available power and potential energy to hit the ball a short distance.

The swing motion should reduce the distance the ball is hit by reducing the backswing energy.

There are three elements that constitute a functional pitch shot swing:

1. Your followthrough will *always* be longer than your backswing.

2. Your body's turning motion, feet to shoulders, will be complete.

Note that there is a completion of the body turn, but an abbreviation of the arm swing.

3. The finish position of your body will look and feel the same as for a full swing except that your arms and clubhead may not generate enough momentum (depending on the shot length) to finish over the shoulder.

Mastery of the pitch swing.
(Using the 3-STEP method.)

STEP 1. SEE the model. Seve Ballesteros, Paul Azinger, or Pat Bradley are great models for this shot. Notice the activity and mobility of their feet and bodies, especially through the hit and followthrough.

STEP 2. SEE yourself as the model. Use a mirror or video playback. Match your motion to the model. Move to Step 3 when your visualized activity matches the model.

STEP 3. FEEL your motion. Feel your sense of *conserve and expend.* Feel your mobility, the lightness of feet and suppleness of turn. Feel the timing of arms and body. Feel the centeredness of hit. See the ball lofting beautifully, landing softly, and rolling gently to your target. Sense the energy used to propel the ball an accurate distance. Sense the energy for different distance pitches. Close your eyes and replay all those senses. Take a moment to amplify your awareness and sensitivity. Thank yourself.

Validation procedure.

Just like with putting and chipping, it's up to you! Just remember to do it.

MORE ABOUT PITCHING

Calibrating distance and response.

How hard you throw a ball, kick a ball, or roll a ball to produce a desired, accurate outcome is wholly a matter of *doing*. The more you do the activity, the more references you store in your brain. A *reference* is the outcome of an experience. The more references you have, then the more refined future responses become. You simply have more memory references with which your brain compares incoming sensory data with stored sensory data. The more you have, the more precise is your brain's charging of muscular activity.

The issue is *practice*. And the issue of practice is one of play. Make practice play. If you love the play,

then you will be practicing at the same time. If you play the game of hit-the-ball-toward-a-target when you go out to practice, then the work of practice will be carried out underneath the PLAY.

Make it *fun*. Go hit the ball for the

fun of it. As long as it is fun you will be attracted and invited to participate.

A few thousand play-shots from now and you will be very accurate. Other golfers will mention how hard you worked. You can just chuckle and play some more.

Three ideas you might want to try.

The fun part of playing wedges is in experimenting to discover all the different distances and trajectories you can achieve with them.

Another experiment is placing your hands lower on the club handle. When you "choke down," you'll see that the ball won't fly as far.

Yet another experiment is opening the clubface (facing it a little to the right). Opening the clubface increases the amount of loft, making the ball go very high. Of course, opening the face also aims it to the right of the target. To then hit the ball straight to the target, align yourself to the left by about the same amount you've aimed the clubface to the right. You are forming a "V" with your stance line and clubface aim with the target bisecting the V. Since you've "split the difference" in clubface aim and body aim, the ball will ignore all that and fly straight to the target.

Always adjust clubface aim *before* gripping the club.

1. *Aim the clubface.*
2. *Aim yourself.*
3. *Grip the club by aiming your hands at the target.*

Looking down, your grip will appear the same as it would for a normal shot.

CHAPTER 12.i
PREPAREDNESS
VALIDATION

Review of the 3-STEP method.

STEP 1. *SEE the golfer that you want to be.* Pick a golfer with your general stature and build. This model will move with a pace and gesture that appeals to you. Observe the model's preparation for striking the ball. Observe the model's manner of movement to the ball, the motion and balance through pre-swing and swing execution. Notice the centeredness of hit and the completion of the swing to a perfect finish position. Note the wholeness of the model's activity from start to finish. Maintain this view, internal and external, until it is the only view you have. When this model becomes omnipresent as your swing model, move to Step 2.

STEP 2. *SEE yourself as the model.* The model has *your* face, clothes, and body. Everything is the same as Step 1 except it is *you* that you see. You are the observer, not the participant. You do not "feel" anything. Continue this observation until you see yourself executing the same activity every time.

PHOTO COURTESY USGA

107

STEP 3. *FEEL the activity. Become the model.* You are no longer the observer or witness. You are now the participant. You now see only what you can observe from the inside-out.

Feel your hands on the club, your approach to the ball. Sense your balance and readiness to swing. Feel the flow of your backswing, the turning of your body, the lightness and mobility of your feet. Feel, hear and see the centeredness of hit. Feel the continuation of your forward motion. Feel the balance and grace of your followthrough. See and emotionalize the imagined flight of the ball in its beautiful trajectory as it flies forward and lands and rolls to your target.

Eyes open or closed, continue this exercise at any place and time. Rehearse the perfection of your golf swing, ball hits, and shots. You are a perfect learner. Indulge in this perfect practice.

YOU'VE GOT IT!

CHAPTER 13 PUTTING IT ALL TOGETHER

Learn from big to small.
Play from small to big.

There are two factors—two separate activities, concepts and mentalities. There are:

1. *Learning golf fundamentals.*
2. *Playing golf.*

These are two different, separate, distinct functions of your brain. The learning of mechanics is, initially, an *abstraction.* The playing of golf is *purely concrete.* The abstract and concrete will merge with its appropriate personal timing for you as you follow the guidelines set forth in previous chapters and subsequent information.

The sequential process for learning fundamentals will accelerate your accommodation of the fundamentals. Practice these fundamentals *away* from the environment of the actual course. Your living room, backyard, garage, office, the park, playground, driving range, putting green, and golf course practice areas are all legitimate environments in which to learn the fundamentals.

Learn the fundamentals from the full swing to the little swing, from the complex to the simple. Continue your learning and mastery from pre-swing to swing to successively smaller and smaller swings.

But play golf in reverse.

110

Assimilate your fundamentals into your game from little to big, pieces to whole, then, play the game from whole to pieces.

Start playing the game by putting. There is NO difference or distinction between practice putting and playing putting. Putting is golf in its purest form. Putting just is.

Putt at the putting green, in your living room and office. Putt at the putt-putt golf course. Putt here, putt there, putt everywhere.

Play the game of little shots (chip and pitch). Play in your backyard. Set up your own miniature chip and pitch course. Use the park or school yard. Go to the practice area at the course and play the game of chip and pitch.

Play the game of full shots. Play par-3 and executive courses. Play on the driving range. Play golf courses which are not excessively demanding of your current skill levels and developing knowledge.

The concept remains the same. Move from small steps to larger steps. Master small things and move to larger. "Larger" is simply the accumulation of smaller pieces.

You will find that your humor and self-esteem remain intact as you assimilate that which you are ready to assimilate. It makes no more sense to play a 7200-yard full-length golf course your first time out than it does to ski the black run your first time on the mountain.

This *is* about play, isn't it?

CHAPTER 14
ATTITUDE
DETERMINES
APTITUDE

And other essential realities.

worth is wholly dependent upon the outcome of the last golf shot.

Sometimes it will be difficult and challenging to step away from all the input and exercise the choice of being your own person, playing golf for your own reasons, and judging yourself from your own criteria. There will be times when the external input will be nearly overwhelming.

But, it's *your* game and *your* creation and *your* recreation. You can choose to see outcomes where others see failure. You can choose to perceive opportunities where others see problems. You can have fun where others work.

The Scots have it right. *Hit the ball, chase it, and hit it again.* There are only two rules they go by: *Play the course as you find it and play the ball as it lies.* The End.

Set the game up so that there is

As beginning golfers immerse themselves in what they believed would be the GAME of golf, they may begin to wonder if it really is a game.

They may find that they are surrounded by serious people who are working hard to survive the "perils and unfairness" of golf. The beginner may listen to a television commentator's account of the "pressure of this testy downhill putt."

If the beginner doesn't discriminate and resist the learned mentality surrounding him, he may believe that the game is vicious and that self-no failure and no expectations. Just love to hit the ball like a child loves to stack blocks. When the blocks fall down there is the opportunity to stack some more—the same or different. *Yippy skippy!*

Learn the fundamentals. Then go PLAY golf. Experience, adjust, experience, adjust, ad infitum...

Yes, there is a "secret" to great golf. It is this: Relish in the good with more zeal, emotional attachment, and genuine involvement than you do for undesired outcomes.

Remember the good shots more than the bad shots and your brain will go in the direction of *good.*

It really is as simple as that. Your brain doesn't care, it will simply go in any direction you send it.

CHAPTER 15
THREE IDEAS

*that are guaranteed to win friends and
influence people (most notably
yourself).*

1. QUICKLY, SAFELY AND
    COURTEOUSLY

Playing golf *quickly, safely and
courteously* is a guaranteed formula
for making friends and influencing
people, lots of people.

Put yourself in the place of the
golf course owner and operator for a
moment. You are standing behind
the counter and in comes Dad, Mom,
and their two young children. You
have one opening in your morning
tee times. There will be 160 other
golfers on the course today, in front
and behind the only opening left for

the day. Now, what do you want to
know about the married-with-chil-
dren group?

Dad, Mom, and kids must be
able to go around your golf course
quickly, safely, and courteously. If
they can do that their money is gold-
en. It doesn't matter how much or little they know about backswings and
followthrough. It doesn't matter if
they know golfing lingo. It only matters that they can "fit" on your
course.

QUICKLY means that you move
fast between shots. Some of the
world's slowest golfers
are very "good" players
but they take half-a-life-
time to hit the shot and
then shuffle onward to
the next. Hit the ball and
get out of the way! Go
hit the next shot. Learn
to play a full-length 18-
hole course in 3-1/2
hours (or less). You may
not be able to do so
every day since there

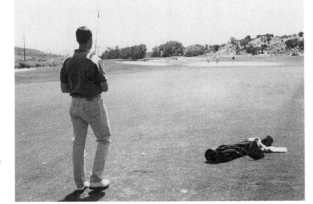

114

will be others in your way!

SAFELY means that you don't endanger other people with your club or ball. Both can cause considerable damage. Know what you're doing; watch what you're doing.

COURTEOUSLY means to be nice to the environment and to the people within that environment. Unfortunately, there are some people that just aren't equipped to play golf. These folks should play tennis with John McEnroe.

For the vast majority of golfers it is a simple matter of being nice to yourself, others, and the grounds. The book *Everything I Need To Know I Learned In Kindergarten* by Robert Fulgum, will be adequate for most golfing etiquette. The remaining etiquette will be filled in by fellow golfers (plus a little more insight that's provided by material in the back of this book). Experience is definitely the best teacher.

2. MAINTAIN HUMOR & ESTEEM

Humor and esteem are much more than esoteric notions or good ideas. Humor and esteem are the core of proficiency.

Humor is the stuff of which creativity is made. Golf shots, once you have mastered fundamentals, are 90-percent creativity and 10-percent intellect.

Humor is the environment of "other-awareness." When you are target-and-conditions-aware, your wonderful brain synthesizes all the available information and draws from its references your best *interaction* with your target.

When you are serious, you become self-aware (self-conscious). You are not interacting with the target. You are acting in a vacuum.

Humor means different things to different folks. In the environment of golf, it needs to mean a lack of self-importance. It needs to mean play, even when the play is extremely focused.

Esteem is a sense of being okay even when the golf ball ends up in a place that is not okay. It is a separation from self and from outcomes such that you are just fine even if your score is not. Esteem is the essential ingredient to experiencing stress without anxiety. Stress promotes the growth of intelligence. Anxiety creates withdrawal from the activity and retards intelligence.

Like the advertisement says: *Just do it!* Nurture your humor and esteem. Golf is a great setting for doing so.

3. CHANGE "PAR" TO SOMETHING THAT MAKES SENSE

This simple little three-letter word has been the ruination of many a golfer. Everything, and most especially a player's sense of accomplishment and esteem, seems to be based around the golfer's relationship to par. Furthermore, our society has taken this term and severely downgraded its meaning. Par doesn't mean "average." It doesn't mean "mediocre." It doesn't mean standard, normal, or reasonable.

Par is extraordinary! It's stupendous! Colossal!

For the record, in golf, "par" is defined as the score an *expert* golfer could be reasonably expected to make on a hole. *Expert* golfer. Unless you play this game for a living, par is not something that you should expect to make, nor is it something that others should expect of you.

The whole concept of par is based around the length of a golf hole. Par is figured with respect to two putts on the green. In other words, if playing a par-4, our expert golfer should take two shots to get on the green and two putts to get the ball into the hole. A par-3 green should be reached on the first shot; the pro's ball should be on a par-5's green in three shots.

Unless you're interested in playing golf competitively, par is a nuisance. Find your own par, and make it anything you want it to be. If you wish to measure yourself against other golfers, you might try using height. On the course, however, if you wish to judge at all, do so by the amount of fun you're having, not by a number.

CHAPTER 16
THERE IS NO SUCH
THING AS FAILURE
Results, outcomes, and congruency.

Golf is playing. In play, there is no such thing as failure.

When you make a swing, hit a ball, or stroke a putt, there will be an outcome to your energy. Something will happen. The result of your experience is just that—a result. Don't let yourself or others define the result in labels like "bad" or "failure." Just use your result as a reference and then try again, allowing the previous result-reference to provide for adjustments to flow freely for the next attempt.

Consider throwing darts. You throw the first dart. The dart misses the board low and right. The experience can be "bad" and humiliating, or it can be what it is—a reference. Your mind-body will made an adjustment and the next dart will hit somewhere else. And so on goes the process until you have stored sufficient references for the results to be refined into more desirable outcomes.

Golf is just the same. *Play* at it. *Experience, adjust, experience, adjust.* Let go of downside judgement.

Just keep playing. As long as it is play then you will find yourself invited to play some more. In all the play, rest assured that your mind-body will make the appropriate adjustments over time.

117

CHAPTER 17
THE FUTURE,
IF YOU WISH

Golf swing you learn early.
Golf you learn forever.

As you are invited into the play of golf, you may find yourself "hooked on it." Millions and millions of people have become hooked. It is quite delightful to be hooked on a game which presents you with a whole series of brand new opportunities every time you're on the course. Something is always somehow dif-

ferent in the environment of the shot. There is, in every shot, the opportunity to be pleasantly surprised, delighted, and gratified with yourself as the co-producer of the shot (the environment is your other co-producer).

Your maturity and knowledge of the game will grow along with your experience. You will learn through your participation, observations, and investigation. Take your time, foster patience, and continually be kind to yourself in a manner which keeps the game a game.

Advice will be forthcoming, whether you seek it or not. The issue is in the way you accept, reject, discriminate, and process your way through the advice so that it serves you and gives you what you want from your participation in the game.

Briefly, the advice about advice is this:

1. Make sure it is compatible with what you want from golf.

2.   Make sure it is intellectually and conceptually understandable and precise.

3.   Be able to accomplish the advice within a few days or weeks and be finished. Validate your mastery of the process.

4.   Keep the learning in the appropriate environment.

5.   Integrate the advice so you can then just *play golf.*

There is more information forthcoming in the next several pages that will give you some ideas on playing the game as well as prepare you against the onslaught of "golfing society."

    Aside from that, however, you are now done!

GO GOLF YOUR BALL.

APPENDIX MATERIAL ▪ ▪ ▪ ▪ ▪ ▪ ▪ ▪ ▪
The second half.

Guide to Appendix contents

Now you're playing golf! Golf is a game, and, as such, it is meant to be played. Not to be studied, analyzed, or, certainly, not to be fretted over. Through your experiences, you'll find your own best ways to get around the course, handle its challenges, and discover everything that you need to continue your progress as a player of the game.

The contents of the following sections, however, will give you a "headstart" on gaining your own experience (or will perhaps help you to better understand your experiences).

a. SPECIALTY SHOTS

The opportunity of challenge.

"Trouble" shots.

Truth is, there really never is any trouble, but that's what you'll hear other golfers call any shot that's not sitting up on a perfect lie. Another truth is that very rarely will your ball ever have a truly perfect lie out on a golf course.

Following are some guidelines for adapting to a few common circumstances. The best "rule" to keep in mind is that overcompensating for the less-than-ideal lie is what causes most mis-hits. In other words, when the ball goes into the sand, rough, or sits on a hill, the amount of compensation necessary to handle the different lie isn't likely to be as much as you might think. Preserving the elements of balance, rhythm, and followthrough will get you through most anything in fine shape.

Sand shots.

Find the easiest way you can to get the ball out of the sand trap.

That criteria is not always going to be answered by the sand wedge. If there's not much height required and if the sand is firm enough that the ball sits on top of it, the easiest way out may be a "normal" chip or pitch shot. If you're pitching, chipping, or even putting from the sand, ignore the sand and just play the shot.

In most bunkers you'll get into, though, your ball will sit down into the sand which makes it necessary to use the sand wedge.

The "sand shot" is very easy to play because the sand wedge is designed to work perfectly in this

Sand traps are nothing to be afraid of! Pros will tell you that the sand shot is really the easiest of all to play because it's the one that requires the least amount of precision in ball-striking. Your intent is actually to hit behind the ball, allowing the sand itself to float the ball onto the green. You'll need only to take a nice, easy swing and finish full.

123

under and through the ball, skimming it out on a little slice of sand. The only time sand shots are difficult is when you try to do "too much" to extract the ball. Just make these few changes, aim, and fire!

Go to a bunker and experiment to see what you need to do when the ball is more or less down in the sand or when there's extra height required. Find out how far the ball will go when the clubhead hits nearer or farther from the ball.

The only other thing you should know before going out to experiment is that you'll probably need to use a bigger swing than you think.

Slopes.

When the ball is above or below your feet on a sidehill, or when you're on a down- or uphill, you need only to adjust your setup and keep a couple of things in mind.

If there's just a little difference between the "planes" you and your ball are on, adjust the height of your grip on the club handle, change nothing else, and swing away. Relax your hands so the club handle is free to raise or lower as you settle into a comfortable position.

If the slope is more severe, then just let your body follow the slope—don't fight it. Level yourself so you're perpendicular to the slope, not to the horizon.

environment. To hit a sand shot, just do this: align yourself a little left of the target, open the clubface a little bit, wiggle your feet down into the sand (choking down on the club to compensate), and swing so as to hit the sand an inch or two *behind* the ball. The heavy clubhead and special sole of the sand wedge will float right

On a down-slope or up-slope, play the ball just a little toward the "back," or uphill, foot and remember that the ball flight will follow the slope. Downhill lies send the ball lower, farther, and a little to the right; uphill lies take it higher, shorter, and a little left.

▓ Don't fight a slope. All that's necessary is a change in your setup. Allow your body to level itself with the slope, not against it. Notice in the above photos how the orientation changes, but the setup looks essentially the same as for a level lie. Allow your hands to shift vertically on the handle to accommodate the change in setup.

On a sidehill lie, play the ball a little bit farther back in your stance, and remember that the ball will fly to the right if the ball is below your feet and to the left if the ball is above your feet. Set up with the slope, aim to account for the ball flight, and swing away.

It's most important to level yourself with the slope so you can swing in balance. Sloped lies are only an alternate perspective from which to play a level shot.

Rough, and others.

From "deep" rough, such as tall grass, get the clubhead on the ball as best you can. If that task looks monumental, use a sand wedge and let the heavy clubhead get down and through the junk. If the ball is really in the deep stuff, sometimes it helps to close the clubface (aim the toe to the left) a little bit when you set up to the ball.

If the rough is relatively light (no deeper than the height of the ball) you can hit a very good shot by simply shifting your stance so the ball is just a little bit nearer your back foot. Don't try to swing differently. It's the effort of trying to get the clubhead "down" onto the ball or to swing extra hard that leads to a mis-hit. Difficult golf shots are "pulled off" through subtleties, not exaggerations.

For a "fluffy" lie in the rough (where the ball is sitting up off the ground), shift your stance so the ball is a little more toward your target foot. Imagine that the ball is sitting on a tee and adjust your setup to match. The ball will fly high but won't have much backspin.

In the rough, don't try to hit the ball too hard. Let your setup do the work.

Sometimes a shot from taller grass is most easily played with a fairway wood. The clubhead on a fairway wood is rounded and has a wide sole; both these things help it "sweep" through the grass and into the ball.

For a hard-dirt lie, or when your ball lands in an old divot, play the ball a little bit back in your stance to make sure the clubhead hits the ball before it hits the ground. The ball will fly lower but will back-spin more.

The driver.

This isn't a trouble shot, but, generally, people have difficulty getting comfortable hitting their driver, or number-one wood. Of all the clubs, it is the longest and has the biggest head and lowest loft. For starters, we recommend that you "tee off," or put the ball into play on a long hole, using another club besides the driver.

Try a 3-wood or 5-wood.

The driver was meant to hit the ball a long way. It was also meant to hit a ball off a tee, not off the ground, so we'll start there.

low, try setting it up higher off the ground; if it's flying too high, tee it "down" a bit and see how that works.

And a good place to start is setting the ball high enough so that the bottom of the ball is in the center of the driver's face (or so that the top edge of the driver's face is at the center of the ball, however you want to look at it).

To "tee up" a golf ball, hold the tee between your index and middle finger with the ball already sitting in the cup on top of the tee. Place your thumb over the ball and use the ball to press the tee into the ground. It's the same sort of "grip" you'd have if you were going to inject the ground with a big syringe.

Playing a shot with a driver requires very much a sweeping motion. For this reason, the ball is positioned further forward in the stance (closer to the target) so that the ball will be swept off the tee.

Adjusting the trajectory of your drive is not exactly brain surgery (unless you believe *other* things you'll read or hear). If the ball is flying too

127

TROUBLESHOOTING GUIDE

If you are consistently hitting the ball such that it does not fly to your intended target, what's happening is that—somehow—either you, your clubface, or your swing path are not aimed congruently at the target. The most common reasons are these: incorrect hand position on the club, neglecting an aiming procedure, or holding a misconception of what is "straight" in the golf swing. Refer to chapters *12.a.1-3* and *12.b.*

There cannot be enough said about the importance of the hands position—

Hands = clubface.

The hands are in control of the clubface throughout the swing. That's why the "grip" is so vitally important to your progress with the mechanics of the golf swing.

The aiming procedure is wholly necessary because, due to your somewhat altered perspective when you're in position to strike a ball, it's tough to tell where the clubface is aimed unless you do so *before* settling in to your address position. One of the biggest foibles is the golfer aiming the stance (feet) at the target rather than aiming the clubface at the target. If your feet are aimed at the target, the clubhead will be positioned along a line that's off to the right of the target. To then hit the ball to the target, either the clubface must be closed down (faced to the left) or the golfer's swing must "cut across" the ball, moving the clubhead from right to left (or from outside to inside the target line). This compounds itself into sliced and/or pulled shots.

There is absolutely nothing wrong with this golfer's swing—the whole problem is in the aim. If you will follow the aiming procedure recommended, this will never be a problem for you.

A golfer will concoct a way to get the ball to the target—that remains the goal or focus. If you wish to get the ball to the target straight away, simply follow the aiming procedure recommended in this book. Likewise, if you wish to develop a mechanically-sound golf swing, then do the same. If you are lined up where you should be, if the clubface is aimed where it should be, and if the hands are supporting the clubface in alignment throughout the swing, there is no choice—the swing will be there!

The reason people have problems with "straight" in the golf swing is because the golf swing is performed on a tilted plane rather than a horizontal or vertical plane as are most other actions in most other sports. "Straight" in golf is sideways-tilted. However, straight is straight. Refer to *Chapter 12.b* and perform the "baseball" exercise until this concept is clearly understood.

Directional problems are very common and are easy to self-diagnose—after you know what to look for. The trick is in first determining how it is that you're hitting the ball right or left. Refer to *Appendix h. Ball flight* for more insight into those things that go bump in the woods.

One more "tip": if you're having trouble making good, solid contact with the ball, try finding a little spot on the ball to focus on rather than just looking at the whole ball. It might be a letter in the logo or the number.

Acceptance by other golfers.	Speed of play.	Inadequate scoring efficiency.	Inadequate distance.	Ball goes right or left.	Hitting behind or topping the ball.	Missing the ball.	Getting started. Fears and limitations.	TROUBLE DO THIS
			•	•	•	•		grip
				•	•	•		stance/ posture
				•				aiming procedure
			•					swing – turn back
			•					swing – turn forward
			•					swish
			•	•	•	•		followthrough and balance
	•	•	•		•	•		centeredness of hit and fit of cluibs
	•	•			•	•	•	focus and attention
		•		•	•	•		clarity/single-mindedness
	•	•						putting
	•	•						chip
	•	•						pitch
	•	•						sand
		•						goal-setting
•		•			•	•	•	patience/ attitude
•	•						•	etiquette and knowledge

129

b. GETTING BETTER

Where to begin the why and how.

Put most of your time and energy into the short game—that is, shots played on and around the green. Whether novice or pro, the place to put your energy is in the putts, chips, pitches, and sand shots.

Why.

• 63-percent of *all* golfer's strokes —your's, your best friend's, your state amateur champion's, and Jack Nicklaus'—are played with less than full swings from on and around the green. Good scores can be generated only through developing shot-making proficiency in close proximity to the green.

• The putts and short shots are *golf.* The target is clear. Your target orientation and interaction with the target is the single most important criteria for the developing golfer. The swing, on the other hand (aka *ball hitting*), can become an unfortunate task of its own, independent of playing golf (interaction with the target).

• Most of golf's rules and etiquette can be learned in the short game. Such preparation brings comfort and confidence to the "big game."

How.

Go to the short game practice area at a golf course. Or use the back yard, living room floor, or office carpet. Putt and chip. Make it as much fun as possible. Play games—one ball against another. Have a contest with your spouse, friends, or kids. Go and find out what all your clubs and all the different ways you can use them will produce for you. Get crazy! Use your imagination. *Imagination is all that the short game is.* Imagination is all that you need to develop a killer short game! The better you can dream up different ways to play the short game, the better you will become, and the more fun you'll have, and the better you will become. What a great cycle!

Suggestion: A great game to play on the putting green is "seven-up." It goes like this: you and any number of accomplices all putt toward a hole on

the practice green. If you "ace" the hole and make the putt on the first try, you get two points. If nobody sinks the first putt, then the one who is closest to the hole gets one point. You each then putt again. If you don't make this putt, you lose a point. The player who scored the point on the previous hole selects the next hole to be engaged. The first player to score seven points wins that round. You can also play out a combination of pitches, chips, and putts using the same format.

When you are on the practice tee.

You will, of course, also rehearse your full shots. After you have learned the fundamental components of the full swing and you are ready to begin hitting balls with your full swing, your practice is now exactly that—a rehearsal.

It is in "hitting balls" that you prepare to play the game. Therefore, your time on the practice tee should be directed toward experiencing the shots you'll hit on the course. Practice as you play: one shot at a time; each shot to a target.

If you find yourself going off in too many directions in search of "what's wrong," stop, get another club and play some more shots with it. Or take a break and go to the putting green. Don't let yourself get caught in the downward, inward spiral of "what am I doing wrong..."

Jack Nicklaus has a wonderful practice routine. Unlike the majority of tour players, Jack doesn't "beat balls." He instead begins his practice with a short iron and plays shots with it until he hits one he likes. Then it's on to the next club up. Sometimes he may hit several balls with one club, but, and this is important, if it happens that the first ball he hits is "It," then that's it. He relishes the shot and moves on. He's got it! (Which is an extraordinary understatement, but maybe this is one of the reasons he has also "kept it.")

You may wish to spend more

time with each club and shot type, and that's probably a good idea for now, but the point remains: always remember that the reason you practice is to prepare to *play*. The purpose of practice is *not* to prepare to continue to prepare mechanically! You've prepared mechanically through following either the 3-STEP or 21-DAY learning methods. On the practice tee, you are collecting experiences and references rather than learning mechanics.

If you hit a "bad" shot, immediately replay the shot in your mind as you would have wished it to be. Take a practice swing and relish in the desirable outcome that you imagine.

Take your time. Take all morning or afternoon. Also important, and this is again related to the purpose of practice, approach each shot as you would on the course. Don't get caught in the trap of haphazard ball-hitting. You're there to play shots, not hit balls. You do not have to be "serious." You must only interact with the

131

environment as you wish it to be and as you find it to be at that moment, which is the fun in itself, which is the game in itself.

Find a target or make one up. You are not out to learn the swing; you are learning to experience the interaction of you, the ball, and target. You are learning to focus your swing to advance the ball such that it produces a desirable outcome. You are out to experience and adjust. You are out to *learn golf!*

Practice your full shots just like you do your short game. Make up games. See what happens. Do it again; do it differently. Just do it. Set your own standards; be your own judge. And have fun!

c. PLAYING THE GAME

If all else fails, try this...

Herein begins the "advanced" information.

As has been explained, it's imperative that you don't add variation until you have completely finished, validated, and graduated through each successive step by whichever learning process you choose to follow. It is critical to your development *especially* not to put Step 4 ahead of the other steps. Doing so ensures, guarantees, and makes certain that you will not reach Step 4! This section, however, contains information that you will become concerned with *after* Step 4 has been successfully completed.

We want this book to serve as your guide to learning golf, a game that, as is fully evident by now, has much less to do with form and much more to do with function. After the form is satisfactory to you, then function begins the game—that is, the game begins...

The wonderful part about following a learning process to its culmination is that, in doing so, you've gotten the mechanics out of the way. Your focus is no longer internal. It shifts to external—interaction with the course and target. After Step 4, experimentation and variation come naturally. When you're no longer worried about how you're doing, then you become entranced with what you're doing.

And what you're doing is finding the best way to get this ball to that hole.

Nothing we can suggest will ever supersede the quality and correctness of what you will determine on

your own. You will find what works best for you. But, we'd also like to suggest a few ideas on hitting different shots, sizing up different circumstances, and offer a few "tips" on playing the game.

Tee boxes.

Give yourself a *perfect* lie. That's a luxury you're always afforded in the teeing area. Since the Rules allow you to place your ball anywhere between the markers on the tee box, take a look at the area and select the best spot to set your ball. You can also move your ball up to one club-length behind the markers, and sometimes doing so might get your ball on a better area. You might also want to consider positioning the ball toward the left or right side of the tee box, depending on which direction you'd like to send the shot.

Course architects sometimes mis-align tee boxes with fairways or greens. Pay no attention to where the tee box is pointing; only know where

that's attempted by far more amateurs than pros. Most people have better success when hitting a full shot (one in which you make a normal swing), rather than a partial shot (one that requires you to adjust the power of your swing). Therefore, unless you are able to reach on or very near the green on the second shot, play that second shot with a club that will leave you with a full swing on your third shot.

Selecting a club.

Most every course has some system that shows the distance you are from the green. These are referred to as yardage markers. They may be small bushes planted on either side of the fairway or stakes that indicate, normally, when you are 150 yards from the green. Some courses also use numbers painted on sprinklerheads that mark more exact distances. Before you play, ask whether the distances are measured from the front or middle of the greens. These markers will give you some indication of which club to hit; however, there are almost always other circumstances (ball lie, slope, wind, etc.) that will dictate the club you choose. You don't want to become a human calculator, but it doesn't hurt to know where you are. Sometimes just the way the land lays makes it difficult to judge distances.

Most players "underclub." That is, they select a club that is insufficient to get the ball the desired distance. The holes on most golf courses tend to be designed so that the "trouble" is situated either in front of or to either side of the green. It, therefore, is often "safer" to hit the ball too far

your target is and line up to that. Do not be distracted from your target.

Par 3s.

The object is to get your ball as near to the hole as simply as possible, which may or may not mean landing it on the green. Generally, try to leave yourself with either level or uphill chips or putts; avoid the downhills and "roller-coaster" areas of a green.

Par 4s.

These are the most common holes on a full-length course. Play your present shot with respect to what you would like to have for your next shot. In other words, visualize playing the hole by looking back from the green to the tee. This strategy will serve you better than any.

Par 5s.

The "long holes." Par-5 greens are designed to be "hit" in three shots, not two. "Going for the green" on the second shot is something

reference for making future plans.

Putting that reference to use on the course comes through making an effort to know how far you need to hit the ball, and then selecting the club that will do that, *plus a little*. The reason for the "plus a little" is because it's not always realistic to count on your Sunday best. This is not negative thinking—it's solid planning that will give you better results more often than not.

than not far enough. Also, trying to "push" a club to hit the ball a greater distance than normal contributes to inaccuracy in both distance and direction. Knowing that the club you have chosen can easily get the ball where you want it to go tends to calm the effort and produce straighter, more predictable shots.

Remember—*centeredness of contact*. That's what matters.

Underclubbing results from a couple of sources that should be ignored. One is from observing other players. The club your playing partners select shouldn't unduly influence your choice. These people may be stronger, weaker, and, remember, also tend to underclub.

Another reason a player might not take "enough" club is because he or she might be failing to account for "averages." As you gain more experience in playing, you'll eventually need to know how far you hit the ball with each club. The best, and maybe only, way to accurately determine that is to "step off" the distance the ball has travelled when you've hit a good, solid shot with a particular club. That distance now becomes a

When you're determining your distance references for each club, pay little or no attention to the yardage markers on driving ranges since they're usually not accurate (and because the ball usually bounces and rolls more at the driving range). Also, since the total yardage on a hole, as listed on the scorecard, is measured from a certain point on the tee boxes, and because the greenskeeper will move the tee markers day to day, you can't accurately judge the distance you achieve by relying on the course yardage markers to tell you how far your ball has gone.

Course "strategy."

Strategy is making a plan for playing a hole. No matter how grandiose or conservative, there is probably no more satisfying thing in golf than "pulling off" your plan.

How you handle any hole mostly relates to exercising your powers of imagination. You really never need to think about this issue; all you really need to do is use your imagi-

135

nation. After a while, and it won't be long, you'll rely less on calculation and more on intuition when deciding how to play a hole. Your intuition, and experience, will be right far more often than not.

It's not negative thinking to say, "John Daly would hit it over those trees, but I think I'll go around them." Play the shot that you have the most confidence in, and with the club that you have the most confidence in.

Make a decision and stay with it. Let indecisions or uncomfortable alternatives run their courses before stepping up to your ball. If a playing partner suggests a shot that you don't feel comfortable trying, just stay with your confidence and hit your best, most comfortable shot. In the long run, you'll be miles ahead.

Many local golf leagues host "one-club" tournaments. In these, the idea is to play a round of golf using only one club. Amazingly, most players will shoot the same scores as they will when using their full sets. And, even more surprisingly, the higher the score a player normally shoots with his full set, the lower the score he'll normally shoot using one club.

Why is this? Simple. You must do the best with what you have before you. There is more creativity required—making one club behave like 14 isn't easy—therefore, more reliance on imagination is imperative. And the more imagination, the better the reality.

Another reason is that there are no expectations made that go beyond the play itself—one doesn't attempt to drive the ball 300 yards with a 5-iron. Play the best shot that seems to be available at the time, and you'll

play many more "good" shots than you will when battling indecision.

When it's possible to do so, playing a "one-club" round is a wonderful exercise in creativity and imagination. Try it on the course, or on the practice range by seeing how many different ball flights and distances you can achieve with each club. You never quit learning golf, not as long as your imagination can see alternatives.

As final advice on "course strategy," look at each hole from the flagstick back rather than from the tee forward. Remember, your present shot is designed to set up the next. Therefore, it's important to first realize the best design for the final shot you'd like to play before making up your mind about what to do on the shots that precede it.

A few hang ups.

Don't let yourself get hung up dissecting holes—make the decision right now to be a player, not an analyst. Look over the lay of the land, note potential trouble spots, and design each shot using your own definition of success. And, perhaps most importantly, should the reality of your imagination go awry, immediately and fully replay the desired outcome—next time you'll "get it."

Don't get hung up on which number iron you're hitting or whether or not you're playing the same club as everyone else is from the tee (most notably the driver). Your score and your enjoyment, and not in that order, are all that matter.

It's a very old, very dusty saying, but it's too true to ignore: *there is no place on the scorecard where you can write down "how," only "how many."*

d. ON THE COURSE
Finally. Fun-time!

This book is about learning golf. It's about playing the game unencumbered by the dictums of The Industry. However, there's a time when you must operate within those dictums. This section deals with what you "need to know" to get on and around a golf course.

A golfer's behavior on the course is under closer scrutiny than the golfer's technique or choice of equipment. This section will prepare you to "act like a golfer," an ability, as you will discover as you employ correct and appropriate behavior, that is sadly lacking from most of the "experienced" golfers you'll encounter. By understanding and using what's in this section, you will set the example.

Although a compete set of "etiquette" guidelines are found in the Rules of Golf, following are a few of the more common courtesies expected of players (and, since there are always certain liberties available in a non-tournament round, we'll also talk about a few ways etiquette can be "modified" to actually become more equitable).

Fast play.
Golf in time for dinner.

In Chapter 12 we offered three simple guidelines for conduct: *play quickly, safely, and courteously.* That's it. If you do those things, you'll be happy and so will others around you. Following are a few more specific ideas on ways these three guidelines may be put to use.

You'll see a lot of pressure directed at golfers to avoid "slow play."

This directive will be printed on scorecards and stickers adhered to golf cars. Warning signs will be posted around the course. Enough will be said about slow play that you'll think it's a felony! And despite all the fervor, you also will encounter six-hour rounds at many golf courses.

What is "slow play"? According to most golf course managers, the "ideal" round of golf is two hours per nine holes, maximum. That pace is considered brisk, but unhurried, by the "powers that be." And it is. Given an open course, meaning that there aren't any players ahead of you, the time to play 18 holes should be no more than 3-1/2 hours.

As a new golfer, you may ask yourself, "how can I be expected to play as fast as an experienced player?" Good question. You'll be hitting the ball a few more times than the par shooter, but after playing a few rounds you'll find out that it's not the time you spend playing your shots that slows things down—it's the time spent between shots (and how that time is used). Follow these guidelines and you'll never worry that you're "keeping up":

1. *Be ready to hit when it's your turn.*

This means that you're at your ball with club chosen and in hand as your playing partner is playing his shot. As you approach the balls, you go to yours and your partners go to theirs (as long as that won't place

anyone ahead of another's ball). After your partners have played their shots, and when it's your turn, play yours straight away.

2. *Play "ready" golf.*

Related to the above, if it's mutually agreed on prior to play, it's a good idea to waive the formality of the "honor" system (meaning that the one who's farthest from the hole hits first). Instead, the one who is "ready" first is the one who plays.

3. *Plan a shot as you're approaching it.*

Don't wait until you're standing over the ball and it's your turn to hit before you decide what you want to do. As you're approaching your ball,

notice where it is on the course, and also notice where the target is located. Think about what you want to do to get the ball from where it is to the target—begin imagining the shot you want to hit. You'll find that this strategy not only results in faster play but also in more productive results. You'll never feel hurried.

4. *Look at the next hole and plan the most "efficient" strategy for getting over to it.*

For instance, always place your bag near the point where you will leave the green to head for the next tee box. If you will chip or pitch the ball onto the green, take your putter with you to the shot rather than playing your shot and then going back to your bag to retrieve your putter.

Not only will this speed things up, it will also result in less "running around."

5. *Don't play "golf car derby."*

If your ball and your partner's ball are on opposite sides of the fairway, it's usually best for one player to pick out a couple of clubs and head on across, on foot, to prepare to play his shot. Do this instead of playing one shot, then loading back into the car, then driving it across the fairway, then playing the other shot.

6. *Don't play "ball mark tag" on the putting green.*

This "game" is part of tournament golf but has no place elsewhere. You'll witness the routine everywhere: Player 1 putts, goes to the ball, marks the ball; Player 2 putts, goes to the ball, marks the ball; Player 3 putts, goes to the ball, marks the ball; and so on and so on. Everyone is playing only one successive putt. As long as you're not going to interfere with the upcoming putt your partner must make (by having to stand on his putting line, for instance), go ahead and "finish" your next putt should you miss the previous one.

7. *Move on to the next tee when you're through putting.*

As with "ready" golf, this practice should be discussed and agreed on prior to teeing off on the first hole. If you have finished putting on a hole, instead of waiting for everyone else to putt-out, go ahead to the next tee and hit away. This keeps things moving at an incredibly fast pace.

And don't stand on or next to the green to mark down everyone's scores. This makes the group behind wait unnecessarily. Instead do all your paperwork on the next tee.

We're not saying to run around the course like it's a foot race. Golf is a slow-paced game, and that's a part of its pleasure. Take as much time as you need to play your shot, but don't waste time elsewhere. That's really all that ever needs to be done to "speed up" play.

And last, but certainly not least, be happy! If you'll notice, the slowest players are those who agonize, stomp, fret, swear, and sulk after each shot. A huge amount of time is wasted in those activities, including, in a worst-case, the time spent retrieving thrown clubs!

Playing through.

If you think that your group is "holding up" the group behind, or if the group behind is in a big hurry, it's a common practice to allow that group to "play through." In this, you will step aside—to a safe place—and either "wave ahead" the group behind or ask them to play through. Let the group hit their shots and get fully out of your way (either outside the distance range of your group's next shots or off the green, whichever the case may be). Conversely, if your group begins to encroach on the one in front of you, if they don't ask you to play through, it's not being "pushy" to request that they do.

Common circumstances include one group losing a ball on a hole and having to stop to look for it; during the time they're looking, another group could probably have time to play ahead. And sometimes it's good practice to "wave on" the group behind to hit their shots into a par-3. Step off the green, let the others hit, and then resume your play when they've hit. In this case, your group isn't going to let the other pass ahead first to the next hole. Instead, you're just giving them the opportunity to hit and move toward the green, and are assuming that your group will be finished with the hole by the time they get there.

Before you let a group play through, or request the same, make sure there is somewhere to go! Decisions should be based on the state of play ahead and behind both groups. Since it takes some time for a group to play through, it just may be that letting one group pass, which means that another group or two has to stand by, will only serve to further hold up play on the rest of the course.

On busy days, most golf courses have a "ranger" who rides around the course in a golf car "directing traffic." It will be the ranger's decision if any group is allowed to pass another. If the ranger tells your group to "pick up the pace," don't start rushing; rather, refer to the guidelines listed earlier and see if you're following them. No matter how many times you're hitting the ball, there's no reason that following the guidelines presented here won't get you around the course in four hours or less. Again, it's always time wasted, rather than time spent, that accounts for delay.

Common courtesy dictates that, especially when the course is relatively uncrowded, reasonable steps should be taken to help everyone play at the pace they desire.

Although foursomes are, technically, always given "preference" on the course, should a twosome in a golf car come up behind your foursome on foot, let them through. Otherwise you'll feel hurried.

If you'll apply a few things in this section, you will soon see that you will be no more likely to "hold up" a group than an experienced player will. It's often the really "good" players who dawdle around the most... Just watch a tournament on television if you want to see some *really* slow players!

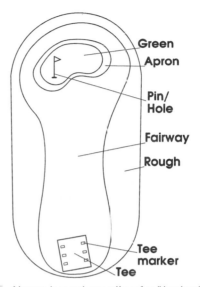

Above is a schematic of a "typical" golf hole (after some experience, you'll find that it's pretty difficult to find any two alike). The tee box is where you begin. There will usually be at least three sets of markers; refer to the scorecard to know which set you should use. The fairway is where you'd like to play your approach (to the green) shots from; it's home to the "short grass." The rough usually gets rougher the further from the fairway you get. Surrounding the green is a yard or so ribbon of grass that's mown about halfway between the grass on the fairway and green. You might ask if the course uses any system to indicate where the pin/hole is located on the green. This knowledge can be important since there may be a few club's worth of distance from the front to back edges of the green.

141

e. PARTICULARS

Good things to know.

Making a tee time.

It's a good idea, and often a requirement, to call ahead to reserve a starting time. And that's all a "tee time" is—a reservation. Most golf courses will take tee times a couple days in advance.

Most starting times are based on 8 to 12 minute intervals. So if you get a time like "10:28" that's the reason. Be on time! The tee time is the time when you are supposed to be *hitting* your first shots, not the time you're supposed to be in the shop paying greens fees.

After playing a while and discovering that tee times tend to become arbitrary figures (because things never stay close to on time at a busy golf course), you may wonder what their function is. Again, a tee time just guarantees you a spot on the course. It's up to golf course personnel, not the golfers, to keep their system on schedule.

Most golf courses are pretty busy, especially on weekends. If you and your partner go to the course as a twosome, the shop will likely "pair" you with another twosome. That may not be an ideal situation, but it is necessary for the shop to try to get as many foursomes on the course as possible. This is done, mostly, to keep play moving at a more even pace. This forced socialization isn't appreciated by a lot of folks, but it is going to happen if the course is busy. If you want to avoid it, you have no choice but to play at a time when the course isn't busy. Mondays are usually best.

You'll find that most people you'll get paired up with are proper folk; you'll probably even enjoy their company. The only challenge is sidestepping the tip-barrage that often accompanies a liaison with new golfers.

You'll probably end up playing most of your golf at one course. Find out what the normal slate of weekly events is so you can plan your play around them. Most courses have leagues, just like bowling alleys do, that are given blocks of tee times on different days. Again, call ahead, even if you don't think the course will be busy, to make sure play is "open."

And one more tip: find out if the course has yearly greens fee deals. If they do, you can usually save a bundle.

You, as greenskeeper.

Help maintain the golf course. It's an old saying, but we can't think of a better one: *try to leave the course better than you found it.* And in general, employ the "golden rule." The next time around, you may become the victim of your own neglect.

Repair your divots, ball marks, and any other "damage" immediately. It takes only a few hours for a freshly-replaced divot or a freshly-repaired ball mark to "heal." Left untreated, it can take weeks.

When you're on the putting green, the only residual damage you are allowed (by the Rules) to repair is other's ball marks. Therefore, if the players before you have been literally "dragging their feet" and have left spike marks, you can't fix them before you putt. You, on the other hand (as well as the player who pre-

As a golfer you have a responsibility to your fellow players: *leave the course in as good shape as you found it.* This obligation is fulfilled by repairing the damage you cause the ground in the normal course of playing your shots.

First, replace the divots that your iron shots unearth (above left). This is simple: retrieve the divot, replace it, and step it back into the ground. And for the record: yes, it's okay to take divots. A divot is an indication of a well-struck iron.

Second, repair the depressions that result from your golf ball landing on the green. This is accomplished by digging out the crater with a golf tee: push the tee in at an angle just outside each of the four sides of the perimeter of the ball-mark, and then lever the tee up and toward the center of the mark. This "fills" back the hole. Tamp it down with your putter and you're done.

ceded you) can repair your own spike marks before you leave the green.

The perimeter of the cup is espe-cially prone to damage. As you remove or replace it, be careful to not bang the flagstick on the perimeter of the hole. And reach into the hole with

143

your hand, not with the putterhead, to retrieve your ball.

Before you hit from a sand trap, take the rake over to the bunker with you (this speeds up play). Use the rake to fill in any holes you've made and to erase your footprints. As with spike marks, the next golfer who lands in that bunker cannot smooth the sand prior to playing his shot.

Handling the flagstick.

When a player is hitting a ball from off the green, the flagstick stays in. When the player is on the green, he may request you to "tend the pin." If you are requested to do so, the golfer wants to use the pin to reference the hole's location. You will stand by, hand on the flagstick; *after* the ball is rolling toward the hole, remove the pin and step aside.

When it's necessary to pull the flagstick and leave it out of the hole, just lay the flagstick on the green a few steps away from the hole. The *next* to last player to putt is the one who should replace the flagstick in the hole.

Getting from here to there.

If you use a riding car, pay attention to what the golf course asks of you in its operation. Keep it on the paths as much as possible and keep it well clear of tees and greens. The areas around the greens, especially, are vulnerable to damage from the cars.

144   Riding cars really should be avoided. These things are not con-

ducive to good play, they really don't speed up play *that* much, and their real function is to make more money for the golf course. Boycott courses that require you to ride.

Instead of riding a car, you might want to use a pull-cart. These rent for very little money and will make walking the course much easier than if you were carrying your bag. If you walk with a pull-cart, they're usually okay to follow you anywhere except too close to the green. Likewise, if you walk and carry your clubs, keep your bag off the apron or "fringe" area of the green; laying it down anywhere else is fine.

Marking your ball.

When you share the green with other players, it's inevitable that one ball will lie in the way of another. When that's the case, the player whose ball is nearest the hole marks its location, picks up the ball, and replaces it when it's his turn to putt. Use a dime as a marker—nothing works better. Sight along a straight line to the hole, place the dime close under the back of the ball on that line, and pick up your ball. Reverse this

procedure to replace the ball.

If your ball lies near enough to another player's putting line, the ball mark itself must be moved to another location. The most common measurement device is a putterhead. First, mark the ball as above, then align the putterhead with something across the green you can use as an aiming reference, and place the mark at the heel of the putter. Reverse the procedure to replace your ball on the green: re-align the putter with your reference, move the mark from the putter heel to its toe, and, finally, replace your ball and lift your dime.

Who hits when.

The term "honor" (as in: *you have the honor...*) refers to which player's turn it is to hit from the tee. The player who had the lowest score on the preceding hole hits first from the next tee; the other players hit in order of their scores. This schedule carries over from the first tee, changing only when the scores on each hole warrant. Determining who hits when from the first tee can be done ranging from a coin toss to whoever says "ready" first.

In the course of play, the player who is farthest from the hole hits first. Don't waste a lot of time on this formality (unless you're playing with those who insist on it) when there are "close calls" to make. If there is no danger potential in doing so, the player who should hit first is the one who is ready. Refer to "ready" golf earlier in this material.

Some people actually measure the distances everyone's balls are from the hole when on the green. This is fine conduct for tournament play, but is pretty silly for a Sunday morning round. Such a procedure involves a lot of ball marking; ball marking is a practice that should be avoided unless it's actually necessary to prevent interference with another player's putt.

Teeing area.

The first step is finding where you are supposed to place your ball. Every golf course has different "sets" of tee boxes. Although it varies somewhat from one course to the next, generally, red markers define the "women's" tee-box, white markers define the "men's" tee-box, and blue markers define the "expert's" tee-box. These distinctions normally relate to the distance from tee to green, with the red markers defining the shortest distance and the blues the longest. Some courses compound the alternatives by adding an extra set of women's markers and sometimes one for the "pros."

You can place your ball any-

145

where between the markers, and, if you want, up to one club-length behind the markers. You're not supposed to place the ball ahead (closer to the hole) of the markers. Also, you are allowed to stand outside the markers to play your shot as long as the ball is between them.

You can *always* set the ball on a tee when you're on a tee box, including those for par-3s where you may be using an iron to play the shot.

"Gimmes."

When a putt finishes so close to the hole that a miss on the next attempt is highly unlikely, it's pretty common to "give" the putt to the player, meaning that you're not going to make him actually play the next putt.

Traditionally, anything "inside the leather" (the length of a putter grip) is given the benefit of the doubt as a "gimme."

Some players jump up and down over their dislike of this courtesy since it is not recognized under any circumstance in the Rules of Golf (and, therefore, is "illegal"). Relax. Giving away putts is a casual-round courtesy that goes a long way toward speeding up play.

The Rules.

The "original" rule of golf was pretty simple: *play the course as you find it, play your ball as it lies.* That has been expanded into an often tangled mess of circumstances, interpretations, and exceptions. You will, at some point (and the sooner the better) purchase a rule book. *The Rules of Golf,* as published by the United States Golf Association, is hardly

engineered for communication. There is another book on the subject that's listed in our *Advised Reading* section, and we strongly suggest that you get it and read it.

The Rules of Golf are not always "against you." In a lot of cases, knowing the Rules may help your game. Unfortunately, most of the Rules *are* out to get you, but they define the game and, aside from common-sensical etiquette breeches mentioned earlier, should always be adhered to.

Without the Rules, we really wouldn't have such a game as golf. You'll see what we mean by that after you've played for a while.

Given the nature of rules, and given the space we have in this book, we can't do them (or you) justice. Don't be afraid to ask "what if" or "what now" of your playing partners. And, again, get a rule book and study it.

By the way, there are many different rules used on the PGA and LPGA Tours. When you're watching an event on television and hear them talking about "line of sight" and other such things, it may not apply to amateur play.

f. GETTING IT TOGETHER
A guide to necessary equipment.

To play the game, you need its tools.
A set of golf clubs consists of several irons, a few woods, and a putter.

Irons, as the name implies, have metal heads. These will be used for the majority of your shots. Each iron has a number, or other identification, stamped into its sole. The larger the number, the shorter and more lofted the club is. For instance, a 4-iron sends the ball farther and lower than an 9-iron because the 4-iron has a longer shaft and a steeper face. The pitching wedge and sand wedges are irons, but are identified by their names rather than by numbers.

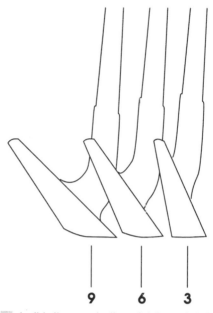

9   6   3

Loft is the angle the clubface is laid back. The less angle, the higher the ball will fly, and the easier the club is to hit. Below is the type of flight a high-lofted club can give (sand wedge).

"Woods" used to all be made of wood; however, it's more common to see them with metal heads. Woods usually hit the ball the farthest of all the clubs. They, too, are numbered like irons, and the numbers indicate the very same things: a lower number has a steeper face and is longer. The number-1 wood is usually called a "driver," while others are called "fairway" woods.

A *putter* is a unique golf club. It is designed to roll the ball along the ground. And there are *hundreds* of variations on the best design to accomplish this simple task. Try them all! But once you have found one you like—stick with it.

Components.
There are a few terms that you'll hear thrown around when people are discussing golf clubs. Unless you wish to become a clubfitter, it's not really important that you understand all their ramifications, but you should know what they mean.

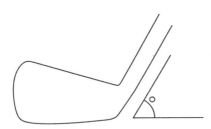

▨ Lie angle. If this critical specification is correct for your swing, the ball will fly straight. If it's not, you'll have to compensate by altering your mechanics.

Loft. Is the angle that the clubface is from perpendicular. The greater the angle, the higher the ball will fly. Very few players need anything other than "standard" loft angles; what is important is that each successive club has an accurate, equally successive difference in its loft angle.

Lie. Is the angle that the clubshaft is to the sole of the club. It is very important that this angle is set exactly to what you need. If it's not correct for you, a "perfect" swing will produce a shot that flies left or right.

Length. "Standard" length for different clubs in your set is calculated from a 37-1/2 inch 5-iron and a 43-1/2-inch driver. Each successively numbered club either adds or subtracts 1/2-inch in length.

Shaft flex. Usually spoken of in terms of "ladies," "regular," "stiff," or "extra-stiff," this refers to the amount of force necessary to make the shaft bend when the club is swung. The harder you hit the ball, the more stiff the shaft should be. If a shaft is too flexible, the ball flight might be erratic. A competent, professional clubfitter can determine what you need, but as a rule, most people tend to get shafts that are too stiff.

Shaft flex point. This refers to the point along the length of the shaft where the flexing originates. The higher (closer to the hands) the flex point is, the lower, shorter, and straighter the ball will fly; the closer the flex is to the clubhead, the higher, farther, and more erratic the ball will fly. This choice, therefore, is a trade-off, but, again, should be left to the judgement of a clubfitter.

Grip size. This is a very important specification. Grips that are too thin or too thick have a significant effect on how well you hit the ball. Your clubfitter will make an accurate measurement.

Weight. There is "swing-weight" and "overall weight." Swing-weight is an arbitrary (meaning that it's not an actual weight measurement) figure that indicates how the weight is distributed, clubhandle to clubhead. Overall weight is an actual measurement, in ounces, of the total weight of the club. These figures do not necessarily relate in coincidence: a very heavy club can, if the weight is adjusted from grip to clubhead, have a very light swing-weight. Most clubs are identified only by their swing-weight (which is a letter followed by a number; "D-2" for instance). Overall weight is more important. Again, let your clubfitter determine what you need.

The decision is now what to get and where to get them.

The "trick" to all of this, as was first said in Chapter 12.d, is finding a *competent, professional* clubfitter. This person could be a local golf professional or a local club-repairman. But find someone who *specializes* in fitting! To help identify this person as such, ask the following question:

Does the clubfitter provide a "dynamic" clubfitting? That is, will he fit you based on the results you experience while you're actually hitting balls under his supervision? If not, if he's only going to measure you as if he were a tailor and you were buying a suit of clothes, find another and ask him the same question.

This is not the be-all and end-all way to determine whether or not a person is a competent clubfitter, but it does indicate whether or not he's got an idea of what is important in helping you play your best.

If the clubfitter will not watch you hit balls and supply you, on the spot, with alternative clubs so you, and he, can judge the results of your fitting, *then you are not getting the attention you need or deserve.*

There are those who will tell you that "equipment doesn't matter; it's the swing that counts..." Do not believe this. Equipment cannot "come later." The equipment must come *now* when you need it most. If your equipment does not fit you, you are lost. You cannot ask your brain to learn a golf swing if the golf clubs will not reward it with the results it deserves. The fact is that the beginner is in most need of properly-fit equipment, and the expert golfer needs perfect equipment the least.

Others (usually salesmen) will tell you that such and such high-trick club will take several shots off your game, and, of course, add several yards to your drives as a bonus. This will not happen.

Walking into a golf-shop today with an eye toward purchasing a set of woods and irons can produce total confusion. There are simply too many clubs with too many gimmicks to wade through.

But the basics of it are simple: the components that really matter are the lie angle, face angle, shaft length and flex, grip size, and weight. These specifications are critically important to developing a natural, powerful swing. A golf club's design idiosyncrasies (such as "perimeter weighting," offset, and shaft material) are not that important.

Following are a few guidelines to assist your interpretations of what you'll hear and see. Memorize these against the onslaught of salesmen and magazine advertisements:

Played by so and so on tour...

Most tour players are paid to play the clubs they use. Most are also given fully custom irons and woods; their clubs are scratch-built to their specifications by the manufacturer that pays them. The manufacturer will not give you this treatment for any price.

Will add yards and yards to your shots...

Many golf clubs that make this claim are simply extra-long and have "strong" lofts (the face angle is steeper). Of course that club will hit the ball farther! In these sets it's not uncommon for their 8-iron, for instance, to measure as a 6-iron by industry standards.

149

Game improvement...

Such gimmicks as "cavity back" irons, "perimeter" weighting, and so on, all promise to produce clubs that are more forgiving and easier to hit. What they are assuming, however, is that you are not capable of hitting the ball on the center of the clubface. But you are. Game improvement clubs have a very dead feel at impact; forged clubs have a very lively feel. Forged clubs, therefore, tell you when you're hitting the ball in the exact center of the clubface; game-improvement clubs probably will not. Your brain cannot produce precise results given imprecise information. Think of forged clubs as "swing improvement" clubs.

Every manufacturer claims to have golf shaft that will launch a ball to the moon and straight as a string all the way there. Whether constructed of space-age this or unobtanium that, golf shafts need only to flex the correct amount and at the correct point for your swing.

Here is another funny thing about equipment combinations: the most popular combination you'll find in most "gadgeteer's" golf bags is a set of offset, cavity-back irons and a set of perimeter-weighted, gold-shafted metal woods.

The first is designed to hit the ball left; the second is designed to hit the ball right. Silly. Downright silly.

Somewhere caught in the middle of this contradiction is the golfer—more specifically, the golfer's brain. The golfer's brain doesn't know any better than to try to hit these two mismatched club designs to the same point; the golfer, on the other hand, wants to have a "consistent" swing.

Golfer and brain just can't get along that way.

Now here's a suggestion that will work...

Properly-fit clubs, while they could be thought of as "custom," do not *necessarily* have to cost a lot of money.

Purchase a set of irons, either used or new, that can be adjusted to fit you. Spend some money (which you will have saved a lot of by doing it this way) on a clubfitting and reworking. Consult your clubfitter before you purchase woods. Again, many of the custom options must be ordered from the club manufacturer.

Watch the newspapers and check the pro-shops (both on- and off-course) for used irons. Another good outlet will be a club-repairman. He'll also be equipped to fit the clubs to you, the service of which can become a part of your "deal."

Which (specific) clubs should I choose?

You are allowed by the Rules to have 14 clubs in your bag, including the putter. The "standard" 14-club makeup is irons 2-9, pitching wedge, sand wedge, putter, and woods 1, 3, 5. It is, however, totally up to you as to which clubs you carry.

Generally, novice golfers will be far and away in a better position if they purchase a "starter set" (a half-set of clubs). Recommendation: 3-wood, 5-wood, putter, and irons 4, 6, 8, PW. This combination is far more utilitarian than the industry's standard starter set of woods 1 and 3, irons 9, 7, 5, 3, and putter. For novice and occasional players, the rule is this: *the more loft, the more better.*

g. BEYOND THE CLUBS
All the other stuff you need.

Golf balls.

Next to clubs, you may have a lot of questions about golf balls.

Here, again, there are a lot of gimmicks for sale. At least, unlike clubs, the ball you choose doesn't really matter that much. Some balls are designed to fly a certain trajectory; others are designed to travel farther; others, still, are designed to produce more "action" (backspin).

These design elements are nearly insignificant. The golfer controls the trajectory, for starters. Most golf balls go the same distance because the United States Golf Association (the folks who brought you the Rules) has set very strict guidelines for how fast a ball can travel as it comes off the clubface. The last, spin, is probably more important than the others.

One ball will spin more than another when there is relatively more weight in the center of the ball than is around its perimeter. The traditional "player's ball," a 3-piece, thin-cover design, will spin more than than the traditional "golfer's ball," a 2-piece, thick-cover design. The first doesn't last as long as the second.

If a ball is offered in different compressions, get the highest (usually 100). For every golfer and every swing, a higher compression ball will go farther and spin more. This information is especially useful for women. Although it may have a harder feel, a 100-compression ball will produce better results for women than an 80-compression "ladies ball."

Our recommendation is to use a two-piece ball, manufacture name doesn't really matter.

Gloves.

Do you need a glove? Probably so. A glove gives a little extra "traction" to hold the club and protects your hand.

Purchase one of the "treated" leather gloves (they're usually advertised as being water-resistant); these will outlast a non-treated glove in an amount greatly disproportionate to its additional cost.

Put the glove on by pulling down its fingers over yours first; don't pull the glove on by its cuff. Gloves are made of very thin leather and may rip if you do that.

Make a fist before you close the back of the glove. If you don't, the glove will be too tight when you grip the club.

If you find that you're between sizes, light-colored gloves usually fit looser than dark-colored gloves.

"Ladies gloves" are usually cut with additional length in the fingers to accommodate long fingernails. If you don't have long fingernails, the glove may not be comfortable. Men's gloves are cut in a much greater size selection, and we suggest you try them on first.

Shoes.

Do you need golf shoes? Yes. Golf shoes are a tremendous asset. They become a "how did I get along without them" item after you've tried a pair.

Buy the best shoes you can afford. Comfort and support are most important, as with any shoes. Generally, an "athletic" style shoe offers more comfort but less lateral support than a more traditional "staff" type shoe. The trouble is that staff-types are not usually comfortable unless you spend a lot of money for the better ones. Very expensive all-leather shoes are the staple footwear on the tours.

If you are in the market for traditional-style shoes, buy leather. There's nothing more to say on that. Synthetics are less expensive and more water-resistant, but unless you're lucky you probably won't be able to find a good fit. If a synthetic shoe is not 100-percent comfortable the instant you lace it up, it will never get better.

Golf bags.

There are a variety of different "carry bags" available, ranging from the simple to the complex; prices correspond. Buy one that has at least a 7-inch diameter top. If it's smaller you'll pull out three clubs at a time.

If you use a pull cart or a golf car, life is easier if the bag will stand on its own. Many carry bags are collapsible. A few also incorporate the use of supports that run from top to bottom in the bag. These bags are ideal for most players since they are light enough to carry and sturdy enough to stand on their own.

Don't fool with those plastic tubes that are supposed to "guide" your golf shafts; they'll come out too and you'll have a real mess on your hands.

And don't waste money on "face-savers" for your irons. The faces won't get hurt in the first place, and in the second place, these things are a nightmare to keep up with.

Use headcovers for your woods. All styles are good, but they're easier to live with if they're not strung or tied together.

A special note for women.

Most "ladies" gear, whether it's clubs, balls, gloves, or nearly you name it, is unfit for good use. It's designed for an "average" woman player (who, according to the equipment specifications manufacturers provide women with, must be somewhere around four feet tall and weigh in the neighborhood of sixty pounds!).

While manufacturers will provide men with a myriad of alternatives, they usually only manufacture one "ladies" product. The unfortunate irony is that there is a far greater variance among women in terms of their physical statures, strength levels, and so on, than is found among men.

Estimates from different sources have claimed that some 80-percent of men play with equipment that's ill-suited to their needs. This figure must be much higher for women.

As is our basic advice for women: in respect to equipment, remember that you are a human golfer, and work with someone who appreciates that. Please don't immediately head, or let anyone lead you, to the "ladies" stuff right off the bat.

h. BALL FLIGHT
What really happened.

If you watch the flight of your golf ball, you will know what happened when the clubhead made contact with it. That is all you need to know to adjust for the next shot. Rather than relying on your intellect, instead let your intelligent brain experience and adjust to produce ball flight outcomes that you like.

Therefore, the following is absolutely NOT meant to evoke your analytical, technical thought processes. Let others "cure" ball flight results based on swing tips. That's not needed. It's much more simple than that...

For a golfer who has a reasonably powerful swing—

• The direction the ball starts out on is determined by the clubhead path at impact (whether it's parallel with or cutting across the target line at an angle toward the left or right).

• The direction the ball then curves is determined by the direction the clubface is pointing (open, closed, straight) relative to the clubhead path. This angle imparts curve-producing sidespin to the ball.

That's it! It is the clubhead meeting the ball, *not* the million and one mechanics that may influence that synergy, that determines the flight of a golf shot. Make the clubhead your ally; make it go where you want it to go. *The ball has no choice but to follow.*

For those who produce less clubhead speed, the "rules" are the same, but there may not be enough sidespin imparted to the ball to have the effect of causing the ball to curve. This golfer can isolate almost all of his or her directional errors to the direction

the clubface is pointing.

Another contributor to ball flight is backspin. Essentially, the more the ball spins back, the higher it will fly and the less it will roll, and vice-versa. More lofted clubs produce more backspin. Backspin helps counteract the effect of sidespin; that's why curved ball flights are more pronounced with the longer, straighter-faced clubs.

(References are for right-handers.)
Shots that go to the right—
Slice. The ball starts to the left of the target and then makes a big curve, landing well right of the target.

Fade. The ball starts to the left of the target and then makes a little curve, landing close to the target.

Push. The ball starts to the right of the target and goes straight, landing to the right of the target.

Shots that go to the left—
Hook. The ball starts to the right of the target and then makes a big curve, landing well left of the target.

Draw. The ball starts to the right of the target and then makes a little curve, landing close to the target.

Pull. The ball starts to the left of the target and goes straight, landing to the left of the target.

The direction the clubface is pointing may further compound both pushed and pulled shots by adding curve. If the clubface is pointing to the right, the push becomes a push-fade or push-slice, and the pull becomes a pull-draw or pull-hook.

153

If you think back to our two "laws," it's easy to see that not all balls that finish to the left are hooks and not all that go to the right are slices. It's also easy to see that it's possible for two shots that finish to the same side of the target to be caused by two totally different reasons. A good example is the push and the slice. In the push, the clubhead is travelling toward a point that's to the right of the target; in a slice, the clubhead is travelling toward a point that's to the left of the target. If the clubface had been closed (pointing to the left) in either shot, the push would become a draw or hook and the slice would become a pull or pull-hook.

Note: Incorrect alignment is going to be responsible for most all of these "problems." Make sure you're following the alignment routine we showed earlier in *Chapter 12.a.3*.

If you're having what you believe are chronic problems getting the ball to go where you wish it to go, or are having troubles centering your hits, we urge you to read *5-Days to Golfing Excellence* and/or view the *Nice Shot!* instruction program. Both were created by Chuck Hogan to facilitate, in part, deeper understanding of the mechanics. See details at the back of this book.

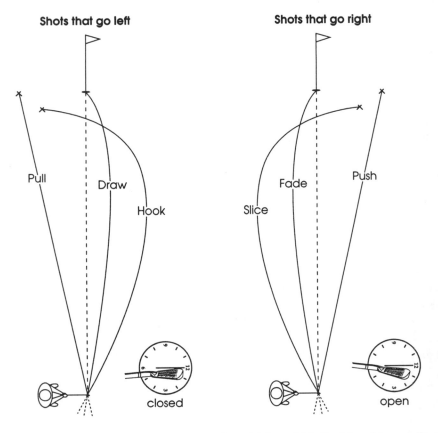

Shots that go left

Pull   Draw   Hook

closed

Shots that go right

Fade   Push   Slice

open

Follow each ball flight line back from the clubhead (dotted lines) to see the clubhead path that caused the ball to start off how it did. The curved flight is caused from the direction the clubface was pointing at impact.

i. CHOOSING AN INSTRUCTOR

The last straw.

If you come to an impasse in your progress, you may be tempted to seek out a professional instructor. Or, at some time in your future, you may wish to incorporate "refinements" into your game. But before you seek out an instructor, review Chapter 12 and take a self-test. Did you really follow the process as outlined? If you did not, then follow the process. It works. If you did follow the process *through* Step 4 for each and every chunk of the instruction in this book, then perhaps an adjustment is in order.

A competent, professional golf instructor is a tremendous ally.

A competent, professional instructor.

But just like "clubfitters" (or "auto mechanics" for that matter), competency is the issue. Professional instruction means, simply, that you're paying for it. Not all golf pros are competent, no more than all auto mechanics are competent. We have prepared a list of questions to ask a prospective instructor.

What percentage of the pro's day is spent teaching?

Giving golf lessons is not necessarily a big part of every pro's duties. Some like to teach, some don't. Find, above all else, one who likes to teach.

Does the pro think it's more important to communicate by feel, demonstration, or explanation?

Hope the pro says "all three."

You will, by this time, have a pretty good idea which means appeals the most to you.

Where did the pro get his or her background in teaching?

While the pro's answer to this question may not really mean much to you unless you're familiar with the "inside" curriculums, listen for name-dropping. If a pro has worked with a "name" golf school or teaching professional, at least you know the pro's been schooled thoroughly.

Find out what the pro's tournament record is.

This will be argued with by many "insiders," including us. Some of the world's greatest teachers are not great players. Likewise, many good players do not like to teach (there's a lot to be inferred from this...). However, if you're not sure where else to start, start with a good player. You know that, at least, the pro's own game is sound.

Who has the pro worked with?

Related to the above, another good indication that a golf professional is a competent instructor is knowing the level of player who seeks out this instructor. If the instructor has a client list of good amateur or professional players, then that speaks highly for his or her reputation.

Finally, don't be afraid to ask for a list of references.

Explain to the pro that you're concerned with finding an instructor who will teach you with respect to your unique learning style. If the pro returns a blank look, infer from that

155

what you will...

Don't settle for any less than a *qualified* professional golf instructor.

The beginning golfer is generally "given" to the inexperienced assistant (apprentice) professionals on staff. The assistant pro is, rest assured, learning as much or more as you are. Don't be anyone's guinea pig. No more than you'd want a first-year medical student to operate on you, don't dare accept an instructor who's in the primary state of his or her own education. Go to the top. If it's a PGA professional, make sure he's a "Class A." If it's an LPGA professional, make sure she's got an "A" or "Master" rating. Although there are many good PGA instructors, the LPGA Teaching Division has a program for their instructors that is very much "people-oriented."

A mechanics-oriented golf school is not necessarily worth the money. Some schools are good, many are not. Learning the mechanics at a golf school, or (worse) at a locally-administered "group" lesson, is contrary to your needs. When working with a group of golfers, the pro has little choice but dole out the instruction in a "one size fits all" manner.

Referring back to what was said toward the beginning of the book, the golf instruction itself is at fault when the student doesn't "get it." Nobody means to give bad advice. There's little intentional evil in the instruction industry. Bad advice stems from two sources: conceptual mis-information on the mechanics and inability to communicate the message, and mostly the latter.

In asking all the questions we've outlined, you're trying to ascertain if the instruction will be conceptually sound, and, even more importantly, whether or not the instruction will be presented to you in a way you can learn it.

If you find an instructor who helps you (and that's by your judgement only), the relationship and experience can be wonderful. There are very few leading Tour players who do not have a professional instructor "on retainer." The truth remains, however, that everyone needs to learn to rely on themselves; do not allow yourself to rely on the instructor more than on your own brain. Through our work with Tour pros, we see this reliance-syndrome repeated over and over again; ironically, it's often these tremendously capable players who succumb to it the most. No matter how good the instructor is, seeking him or her out at every turn becomes a crutch that will eventually let you down hard.

Learn what the pro can give you and then bid formal instruction farewell. Get on with the game. *School's over—GO PLAY!*

Note: Whatever the pro tells you to do, and provided that you choose to follow his or her advice, please use either the 3-STEP or 21-DAY learning methods (as well as the Goal-Setting Process, if you wish). You might want to ask the pro if you can video-tape his or her golf swing to use as a model.

j. GOAL-SETTING PROCESS
(for the *really* motivated golfer)
A map for getting where you want to be.

A goal is a destination. To benefit from goal setting, you must follow a process that allows you to determine exactly where it is you want to go, determine exactly how you will get there, and determine how you will know when you have arrived. And along the way you must also take the time to re-evaluate this road map. You may find that you've taken a wrong turn, gotten yourself lost, or, perhaps, started down the wrong road to begin with.

1. Make a list of goals. Make no judgments as to what you believe you are capable or not capable of achieving. Simply list those goals that seem fun and satisfying to you.

2. Select and list three of the most important goals you wrote above according to their priority of importance to you.

3. Through imagination, fantasizing, and daydreaming, consider what impact the achievement of any one of these goals will have. What will be satisfying about the achievement? What are the implications and the impact of the achievement upon your life?

4. Rank the goals again according to priority or replace goals as desired after Step 3.

5. List the date the goal will be achieved: day, week, month, year?

6. List the current assets and resources (internal and external) you possess that will help you achieve your goal.

7. Identify and list the potential limitations that have impeded you in the past or may impede you in the future.

8. List resources and people who can assist in your achievement and increase the breadth of your resource base.

9. List the specific actions you will take on a daily and weekly basis to move toward reaching your goal.

10. List the actual time and action you will allocate daily. (Include the specific time of day if appropriate.)

11. From Step 5, list three different dates on which you will evaluate your progress as you move toward your goal achievement date. (For example: If

the achievement date you named in Step 5 is one month from the day of commencement, then you would review commitment and followthrough at the end of each week during that month.) Make necessary adjustments in Steps 9 and 10 after establishing your progress checks.

12. Acknowledge and reward yourself for the achievements and commitments that you have accomplished during the stated time period. Validate and claim every success you have, regardless of how small.

13. List the actual outcomes and results that were or were not achieved when the predetermined time period elapsed.

14. Review the entire process, Steps 1 through 13.

15. Evaluate your goals and adjust or replace them as necessary. Ask yourself:
    a. Was it really my goal or was it one that others set for me?
    b. To what extent do or did I really want that goal? Was I really motivated to reach it? How important is it?
    c. How will the attainment of the goal actually satisfy me?

16. Do it all again. Repeat the whole process. Realize that it is the precision of the process that sends your brain in the precise directions which will yield the desired results. It is NOT that you fail. It is only that you have yet to become as precise as you will become through experience, adjustment, experience, adjustment, experience...

17. Dwell upon the good that you have done in following this process. Those areas and elements that are lacking need to be reviewed once and once only. Those areas and elements which you master must be acknowledged, validated, and personally owned by you.

k. ADVISED READING AND INSTRUCTION MATERIALS

Materials by Chuck Hogan

Books and booklets
> *Learning Golf*
> *Five Days To Golfing Excellence*
> *Practicing Golf - A System For Generating the Best Golf That You Can Play*
> *Goal Setting, Preparation, and Performance Calendar*
> *The Magic of Imagery*
> *Magical Child Synopsis*
> *Golfers Resource Handbook*

Videotapes
> *NICE SHOT!*
> *Insight to Great Putting*
> *Yoga Exercises for Better Golf*
> *The Player's Course (a multi-media mix of video, audio, and print for self-development by experienced and expert golfers)*

Audiotapes
> *Self Hypnosis For Better Golf,* plus *Yipnosis*
> *Exercises For Golfing Excellence*
> *Peak Performance Imagery Cassettes*
> *Twelve Means To Lower Scores*
> *How To Practice Golf*

Materials by others
Armour, Tommy, *How to Play Your Best Golf All of the Time,* 1985, Ailsa.
Bandler, Richard, *Magic in Action,* 1984, META.
Bandler, Richard, *Using Your Brain for a Change,* 1985, Real People Press.
Bandler, Richard and Grinder, John, *Reframing,* 1982, Real People Press.
Bandler, Richard and Grinder, John, *Trance-Formations,* 1982,
> Real People Press.
Bandler, Richard and Grinder, John, *The Structure of Magic II,* 1976,
> Real People Press.
Boomer, Percy, *On Learning Golf,* 1946, Knopf.
Gallwey, Timothy, *The Inner Game of Tennis,* 1979, Bantam.
Garfield, Patricia, *Creative Dreaming,* 1976, Ballantine.
Gawain, Shakti, *Creative Visualization,* 1979, Bantam.
James, Jennifer, Ph.D., *Success is the Quality of Your Journey,* 1986,
> Newmarket Press.
Korn, Errol R. and Johnson, Karen, *Visualization: The Uses of Imagery in the
> Health Professions,* 1983, Dow Jones-Irwin.

159

Knudson, George, *The Natural Golf Swing*, 1989, McClelland and
    Stewart, Inc.
Leadbetter, David, *The Golf Swing*, 1990, Willowbooks
Leonard, George, *Ultimate Athlete*, 1975, Viking.
Maltz, Maxwell, *Psycho-Cybernetics*, 1968, Wilshire.
Murphy, Michael, *Golf in the Kingdom*, 1973, Dell.
Murphy, Michael, *The Psychic Side of Sports*, 1979, Addison-Wesley.
Pearce, Joseph Chilton, *Magical Child*, 1979, Bantam.
Watson, Tom, *Rules of Golf*, 1992, Simon and Schuster.

I. GLOSSARY

The following is not presented in alphabetical order.

GENERAL TERMS

Golf. A game.

Golf course. A place to play a game.

Player, golfer. Look in the mirror.

Esteem. What you think about yourself. If you're a player of golf, think very highly of yourself.

Humor. A state of mind in which there is no awareness of self.

Neuro-_____. Means "brain." Neuro-technology, for instance, means technology, or techniques, which deals with the brain (and with learning).

Failure. By your definition only.

Success. By your definition only.

Greens fee. The charge (fee) to play a course (the greens)—not "green fees." Always too much, but always worth it..

Greenskeeper. The person, or persons, responsible for maintaining the golf course.

Starting time, tee time. A reservation for play. Always get one by calling one or two days prior to play. And be on time—the tee time you get is the time when you're supposed to be hitting your first shots off the first tee.

Ranger. A person who rides around the golf course when the course is crowded. The ranger is supposed to keep play moving at an appropriate pace.

Scorecard (don't forget the little pencils). This is the form you fill out to count up your shots. Even if you don't want to keep score, the cards usually have some good information about each hole (length, diagrams, etc.).

PGA. Professional Golfers Association. Two branches: club pros and tour pros; the first are golf professionals and the last are professional golfers.

LPGA. Ladies Professional Golf Association. Two branches: club pros and tour pros. Same definitions as above.

161

S.E.A. Sports Enhancement Associates, Inc. A small group of individuals who push humor and esteem.

Tour. A professional tournament circuit. A tour pro, or touring professional, is one who plays on it.

USGA. *United States Golf Association.* The bunch that governs amateur play and writes the Rules of Golf.

SCORING/PLAYING TERMS

Stroke. An attempt, whether successful or not, at striking a ball. Count up all the strokes you take to get around the golf course, and that's your score.

Par. The score that an expert golfer should make on a hole. Par refers to each hole individually, and par for the course is all the pars for all the holes added together.

Birdie. One under par on a hole.

Bogey. One over par on a hole.

Course rating. Used by the USGA in determining handicaps. Not all courses are of equal difficulty. The course rating number tells you a lot about the course you're about to play (a high rating—high number—means a more difficult course).

Handicap. For those interested in competitive golf, a handicap (given by the USGA) reflects the number of strokes you are "given" prior to play. For instance, an 18-handicap gets to subtract one stroke per hole from his score.

Foursome, twosome, etc.some. However many are in your playing group. If it's you and your partner, tell the shop-person you have a twosome. Try to get three friends to join you so you'll have a foursome. That's about the only way you can play with people of your own choosing.

Honor. In golf, this refers to who has the "right" to hit first, determined by the lowest score on the last hole or holes.

Away. As in "you're away," refers to the player whose ball is furthest from the hole. Unless agreed on prior to play, this player always hits before the others in the group.

162

Etiquette. Essentially, in golf this refers to how you should behave on the golf course.

TYPES OF SHOTS

Hook. A ball that makes a big curve to the left.

Draw. A ball that makes a small curve to the left.

Pull. A ball that starts to the left and stays to the left; the ball flies on a straight line.

Pull-hook. A ball that starts to the left and curves farther to the left.

Slice. A ball that makes a big curve to the right.

Fade. A ball that makes a small curve to the right.

Push. A ball that starts to the right and stays to the right; the ball flies on a straight line.

Push-slice. A ball that starts to the right and curves farther to the right.

Shank. This is a shot that is hit off the hosel of an iron.

Topped or bladed shot. This is when the ball is hit above its centerline by the leading edge of the clubface, causing the ball to roll instead of fly.

Fat shot, or chunk. This is when the clubface hits the big ball (Earth) before the little ball (golf).

COURSE TERMS

Flagstick, pin. The pole that sits in the cup to show you where the hole is located.

Hole, cup. The object of your affection. It's a round hole in the ground that's 4.5 inches in diameter. Put the ball there.

Fairway. The more closely-mown area between the tee box and green. This is where you want to keep your shots.

Rough. The less maintained area between the tee box and the green. Depending on the part of the country you live in, and on how far from the fairway your ball is, the rough will be more or less difficult to play a shot from.

163

Bunker, trap. These are little pits situated around the golf course. Usually filled with sand, but occasionally will be of deep grass.

Cart path. An annoying maze of roads for riding cars to follow.

Fringe or apron. The area right around the green that's usually mown shorter than the fairway but not as short as the green. You can play any club from the fringe as you are not considered to yet be on the green.

Green. The closely-mown area on each hole where the flagstick and hole are located. Be careful to not damage this smooth surface.

Tee box, tee markers. The designated place on each hole where you hit your first shot from. Usually marked like so: red (forward), white (middle), and blue (back).

Yardage markers. These are shrubs, stakes, signs, or a combination, that indicate how far your ball is from the green. Look on the scorecard to know what they are and what they show you. Also look for markers placed on the ground, sometimes on sprinklerheads.

Divot. A little patch of earth and grass that gets sliced out of the ground on an iron shot. Pick it up, put it back. It will grow again.

Ball mark. A depression left by a golf ball landing on the green. Fix it.

Pro shop. Your first stop when you get to the course to play. Go to the counter and check in, just like at a hotel.

Starter. Some courses have a person whose job it is to organize the order of play from the first tee. If so, the person in the golf shop will give you a ticket to present to the starter when you arrive at the first tee.

Driving range, practice tee. An area for warming up and testing fundamentals. Not to be confused with "golf."

Practice green. An area for warming up, testing fundamentals, and learning golf. Make sure you ask if it's okay to chip onto the practice green; some courses have a separate area for this practice.

Par-3 course. This is a great place to start. As implied, a par-3 course is a layout, usually of 9 holes, that consists of only short holes.

Executive course. This is one little step up from a par-three in that it may also have some longer, par-4 holes.

164

Regulation course. This is a "full-length" golf course, usually consisting of 18 holes (you can play 9 or 18). This is the final step. Also, there are vast and great differences among regulation courses: some require much more or less skill to negotiate, just like ski runs.

Pars: 3s, 4s, 5s. Unless there are extenuating circumstances, such as the layout of the hole, golf course designers generally go on distance alone to determine par for a hole. Generally, a hole shorter than 250 yards will be a 3-par; from there up to about 450 can be a par-4; beyond that are par-5s.

Putt-putt. Fun-fun. Watch out for the windmill!

RULES TERMS

OB, out of bounds. Avoid this. If your ball goes there, you're cooked by the Rules. Defined by white stakes.

Hazard. Different from a trap or bunker. A hazard is normally filled with water, but not always. Specific rules apply to what happens after your ball lands in one.

Ball mark. A way to indicate where your ball was on the putting green in the case that its position interferes with the line of one of your partner's putts. Comply if asked by one of your playing partners.

Through the green. This is the area between the tee box and the green. It includes the fairway, the rough, traps, and hazards. Many of the rules use this term and you'll hear others mis-use it.

EQUIPMENT TERMS

Clubs. The implements with which you play the game of golf. You can carry 14. A club is any golf club—putters, woods, wedges, and irons.

Iron. One of many metal clubs in your bag. You'll use these most often.

Wood. Although not necessarily made of wood anymore, these are the clubs that have larger, rounded heads than the irons.

Driver. The number-1-wood. This is a big-headed wood designed to hit a ball from off a tee.

Fairway wood. Woods that are designed to hit a ball from either the ground or from a tee. A 3-wood is a very effective driving club.

165

Putter. The most important club, and shot, in golf. Try them all and then keep the one you choose forever.

Wedge. Irons that are designed to hit the ball higher and a shorter distance than the other irons. They are what you use when you're in need of such a shot.

Clubhead. The whole thing that's stuck on the heavy end of the shaft.

Clubface. The part that hits the ball.

Heel/toe. Just like your foot. The heel is nearest to the clubshaft (leg).

Hosel. The part of the club that comes up from the heel and surrounds the clubshaft.

Shaft. The long flexible part of the club.

Sticks. What some folks call golf clubs.

Tee. A wooden peg designed to hold your ball on the teeing area. Place the ball on the tee first before you drive the tee into the ground.

Carry bag. A lightweight "collapsible" bag with a shoulder strap, designed to be light enough for the golfer to carry around the course.

Golf cart. Really should be called a "golf car." This is a motorized (either gas or electric) contraption designed to haul people around golf courses. In Scotland you usually need a doctor's note to drive one; in America, you usually need a Congressional favor to avoid one.

Pull cart. A brilliant alternative to shoulder-carry and cars. This is a two-wheeled contraption that holds your golf bag and is pulled along behind you. Rent for pocket change or buy your own for somewhat more.

Spikes, nails. Cool-talk for golf shoes.

ABOUT CHUCK HOGAN

Chuck Hogan, author of *Learning Golf* and founder and president of *Sports Enhancement Associates,* is the most successful coach on the professional golf tours—and is perhaps the most effective coach for golfers of all abilities. His professional client list reads like a who's who of top money winners: Peter Jacobsen, John Cook, Johnny Miller, Colleen Walker, Cindy Rarick, Duffy Waldorf, D.A. Weibring, and the list goes on. All totalled, Chuck has worked with over 60 professionals on the PGA, LPGA, PGA Senior, and Ben Hogan Tours. More importantly, Chuck and S.E.A. have helped thousands of amateur golfers of all abilities play better, more satisfying golf.

Chuck is a leader, an innovator, a renegade!

He began his study of performance after the frustration of teaching as a PGA professional golf instructor left him wondering why some of his students could "get it" and why others couldn't. Chuck knew that everyone had the ability to "get it." So he went to work, and a few years later, he found "it." The answer was simple: Everyone can "get it," given the right direction—and everyone needs a different direction.

Working through the limitations of the golf instruction industry left him no place to go. It was the "institution" itself that had constructed the barrier to most people's enjoyment and success in golf.

In 1984 be founded S.E.A. and began working on his own. Tour players began flocking to him, and they began winning.

The word spread, and today there are thousands of golfers, amateur and professional, who are applying Chuck's concepts.

In addition to *Learning Golf,* Chuck has created numerous, leading-edge instructional programs and is a frequent contributor to several magazines.

**WE ARE GRATEFUL
TO THE FOLLOWING PEOPLE**

Steve LeDonne, for actually encouraging us to run crazy on his golf course, Rifle Creek Golf Club, Rifle, Colorado. That's where we took photos.

Teresa Manupella, for agreeing to be in some of those photos, and for making them much more attractive as a result.

And a very special thanks to my friends and true golfers—
        Mr. and Mrs. Edward and Francis Page.

WHAT'S NEXT?

Assuming you're now hooked...

On the following pages are four special programs created by Chuck Hogan, the author of *Learning Golf* and president of S.E.A.

These materials are highly recommended to add to your knowledge and depth of understanding of the golf swing, short game, personal performance strategies, and *playing the game of golf.*

What is S.E.A.?

S.E.A. means *Sports Enhancement Associates.*

Our name is what we do.

S.E.A. is dedicated to increasing the level of human performance. We're best known for our work on the professional golf tours, but through our schools and products, we've helped countless amateurs of all skill and experience levels score better and enjoy golf more.

If, after following the plan outlined in *Learning Golf,* you'd like to develop a deeper understanding of all that's associated with superior golf performance (and enjoyment), S.E.A. has all the tools you need.

In your experiences with other golfers who didn't have the headstart that you've just gotten, you are likely to encounter a few who could really benefit from S.E.A. concepts. They're easy to spot—you'll find them out on the range, beating ball after ball, taking lesson after lesson, and having nothing to show for it but sore hands and an empty wallet. Please share what you've learned with them, and tell them about S.E.A.

In addition to the products listed, we also recommend our *Goal Setting Calendar* to help keep your progress moving forward. Our *Golfer's Profile System* is a fun, easy to take self-test that will reveal your preferential learning style; this valuable knowledge will allow you to formulate your own best strategy for benefitting from future instruction (whether it's hands-on or self-study).

We even have a specific program designed especially for experienced golfers who are not getting what they want from the game—our award-winning *The Player's Course.*

While many will tell you that that the answers to great golf are found in better mechanics, more practice, and harder work, you've learned that the answers are really found in *finishing* the mechanics, *better* practice, and harder *play.*

S.E.A. can show you how to make the most out of what you've got, and we can show you how to get *exactly* what you want to have. S.E.A.'s method isn't another swing theory and it's not "sports psychology." It's the first system that goes directly to the root of playing better:

S.E.A. will show you how you learn.

It is what you *do* that counts.

S.E.A. breaks down the barriers, limiting beliefs, and confusion of golf instruction so you can move quickly and permanently to becoming the player you want to be.

Analysis is worthless without action. S.E.A. instruction isn't "all theory." After all: It isn't what you know that counts—it is what you *do* that counts!

And what we do is this:
We teach golf...

169

NICE SHOT!

by Chuck Hogan

This is it! The original. The program that set a new standard for golf instruction! A recent survey of 3000 golf professionals voted *Nice Shot!* as the best golf instruction video they'd ever seen!

We recommend this program if you wish to add to your depth of understanding and comprehension of both the mechanics of golf and their ultimate integration into *play.* And, of course, the video presentation adds a totally different angle to the message. *Nice Shot!* will show you the difference between playing golf and playing golf swing. If you want to play golf, this program is for you.

The central video tape takes you through the form and process of learning mechanics—for good. The audio cassettes and playbook will assist you in understanding how to convert mechanics into low scores. With *Nice Shot!* you don't have to piece together your game. Mechanics, comprehension, and then conversion (to low scores) are each detailed and then integrated.

This instructional program is designed for golfers of all experience and ability levels.

Cost, $59.95

★★★★★ *"This fascinating video is the first to break out of the 'here-is-how-to-hit-a-shot mold' ... and teach a better way to learn."*
—*GOLF* magazine

to order, call toll-free
1-800-345-4245
credit cards accepted

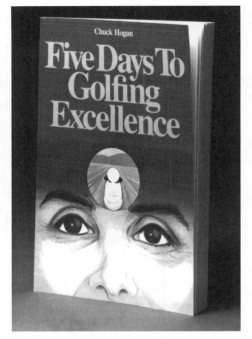

FIVE DAYS TO GOLFING EXCELLENCE

by Chuck Hogan

This 162-page book is a five-day self-study course on golf swing mechanics and playing the game.

We recommend *Five Days* for those who wish to dig a little deeper into the "science" of great golf.

Each of its five chapters of is meant to be read one day at a time.

On day-one you'll learn how to eliminate tension on the course and make learning golf a sequential process. On day-two the swing mechanics are presented in a simple, easy to understand manner.

Subsequent days provide new insights and information: how equipment influences the swing, imagery techniques to accelerate learning, preshot routines that always trigger your best shots, mental mechanics, and diet and exercise plans.

Published in 1985, *Five Days to Golfing Excellence* is the foundation for Chuck's future works. A must for anyone interested in Chuck Hogan's concepts.

This book is designed for golfers of all experience and ability levels.

Cost, $11.95

"Don't just read this book—use it!
This is what they don't teach you at any golf school."
—Mark H. McCormack, the author of *What They Don't Teach You at Harvard Business School*

to order, call toll-free
1-800-345-4245
credit cards accepted

12 MEANS TO LOWER SCORES

by Chuck Hogan

You hit the ball well on the driving range, yet once you get out on the course, your results are nowhere near your expectations.

If that sounds familiar, this package is for you. *12 Means* is designed to help overcome the barriers that keep you from reaching your scoring or playing potential.

If you feel that you've learned the mechanics to your satisfaction but are unable to convert them to satisfying play on the course, we recommend that you give this a listen.

This two-tape, 140-minute audio package features Chuck Hogan addressing an audience of tour pros and dedicated amateurs.

You'll learn to replace doubt with trust, how to develop triggers for playing consistently great shots, and how to discern good instruction from bad.

Every listener is guaranteed new means to improved play! And if you're a commuter, you'll enjoy the easy-listening format.

This product is designed for golfers of all experience and ability levels.

Cost $19.95

to order, call toll-free
1-800-345-4245
credit cards accepted

PRACTICING GOLF:
a system for generating the best golf you can play
by Chuck Hogan

This 53-page book and 45-minute audio transcript explains exactly how to convert practice energy to scoring proficiency.

We recommend this program as a companion to *Learning Golf* as it will give you the means necessary to guarantee success in your personal mastery of golf.

You'll learn:

- Strategies for scoring consistency.
- The most important, and most neglected, shot in golf.
- A complete analysis of what and how to practice.
- Mental practice for mental toughness.
- Using data and records to make efficient shifts of practice energy.

If your only reward for working your fingers to the bone is bony fingers, then this is for you!

Our professional clients think that this package is one of the most effective educational tools in golf.

This package is designed for golfers of all experience and ability levels.

Cost, $19.95

"This is THE means to convert from hitting to scoring. You will never again have to repeat those disgusting words 'well I hit it good but didn't score.' Why not practice smart?"
—Chuck Hogan

to order, call toll-free
1-800-345-4245
credit cards accepted